SPLASH THE LIVING WATER

ESTHER BURROUGHS

A JANET THOMA BOOK

THOMAS NELSON PUBLISHERS
Nashville

AUTHOR'S NOTE: The names of the people used in my illustrations have been changed to protect their identity and confidentiality.

Published in Nashville, Tennessee, by Thomas Nelson, Inc.

Library of Congress-in-Publication Data

Burroughs, Esther
    Splash the living water / Esther Burroughs.
      p.   c.m.
    ISBN 0-7852-6958-4
    1. Christian women—Religious life. 2. Female friendship.
  I. Title.
    BV4527.B8694 1994   98-53423
                                                     CIP

Printed in the United States of America.

6 7 8 9 10 – 04 03 02 01 00

To

Bob L. Burroughs, my precious husband.
Thank you for the hours you spent finessing
my manuscript, and even more, for Christ's
love in you that has splashed my life with
His presence through your gentle
touch for forty-some years.

CONTENTS

Acknowledgments
vii

1. And She Was Thirsty
1

2. Accepting the Water
15

3. Keep Coming, Keep Drinking
30

4. Intimacy Through Prayer
46

5. Clothed in the Spirit
61

6. The Wellspring of Family Worship
86

7. Sharing the Dipper
115

8. Soaking Up the Interruptions
139

9. Splashing the Living Water
169

About the Author
195

ACKNOWLEDGMENTS

I would be remiss if I did not express my gratitude for the joy of serving eleven years as consultant for Women in Evangelism for the Home Mission Board (now the North American Mission Board). During this time, I developed a seminar called Lifestyle Witnessing for Women. The seed thoughts of this book were developed while teaching the seminar.

I am grateful to: Terry Meeuwsen, new friend and sister in Christ, for suggesting to Janet Thoma that she invite me to write for Janet Thoma Books; Robert Wolgemuth, my literary agent, for making it happen; Janet Thoma, my editor, for carefully crafting and enhancing my written voice, and sharing grandmother stories; to Melody Reid, my wonderful assistant, for her prayers and detailed work related to the writing; Nicole Johnson, actor and author, whose constant, encouraging voice kept me writing; my Monday prayer group, who prayed me to the computer day after day and rejoiced as each chapter was finished; my family members who cheered me on as each chapter was completed; and to the Thomas Nelson family, new friends, for the pleasure of working together.

1

AND SHE
WAS THIRSTY

The early afternoon heat hung like a damp blanket in the air. Yet the task ahead kept her feet plodding wearily toward the well at the edge of the village. She was aware that everyone in the village of Sychar knew her story. It was, perhaps, their story. The well was the town's gathering place. Jacob, a local hero, had bought this property and had given it to his son. This well had watered Jacob's family, his cattle, and his workmen. The well now belonged to the community.

I wonder, did she ever think about the God who provided this well and the care it gave His people? She had made the journey to the well many times. Some days, perhaps, she wished the time would come when she would never have to return to the well. She did not like to visit the well, and she dreaded the trip every time she had to go. But the journey was a daily one for every woman in the village.

The time at the well was a time of community for the village women to share family news and events . . . visiting about family, foods, husbands, children, and a time to gossip! (Remember those times when you had to do your laundry at the local laundromat!)

But the village women's community had no place for this Samaritan woman. She had few, if any, friends because of her lifestyle. She was, perhaps, sleeping with a husband or a boyfriend of one of the women. She knew they called her "the Samaritan woman." Most women went to the well in the cool of the morning. But to avoid their gossip and stares, this woman went at noon . . . when it was very hot.

Did the women in her city have any idea of the nagging emptiness of her life or of her personal thirst? Did any of them ever wonder about her loneliness? If anyone had asked her about her needs that day at the well, she might not have been able to answer. What was she seeking as she moved from relationship to relationship and from man to man? Did she want children? Was she longing for a close friend? Maybe she desired a family and the opportunity to belong to a real community. Or . . . maybe it was just another day of drudgery getting water for common household chores.

Hear her story. Jesus, weary from His long journey, was sitting by this well to rest. He was tired . . . and thirsty. At His request, the disciples had gone into the village to buy food for their meal.

Jesus must have cherished this moment alone. Approaching footsteps interrupted His thoughts. Seeing the Samaritan woman, Jesus said these simple words to her as she began to draw water from the well: "Give me a drink."

The woman replied, "How is it that You, being a Jew, ask me for a drink, since I am a Samaritan woman?" She knew the rules. She understood the mandate. In that day, men did not speak to women in public, especially at the town watering hole! In addition, Jews had nothing to do with Samaritans—period. And to get a drink of water one had to have a dipper, and Jesus had none.

Jesus' answer was gentle and inviting. He explained that He was the "gift of God," and if she asked, He could give her "living water." She must have looked Him over very carefully, unsure of this request, and at the same time, aware that He did not have a dipper with which to draw the water. Was she thinking about the depth of the well—perhaps as deep as her troubled life? Even in her concern about His lack of well-drawing equipment, she seemed to be drawn to Him—yet she was confused by the truth of His words. Choosing to rush on, she asked Him this question: "Where . . . do you get that living water? . . . You are not greater than our father Jacob, are You?" (John 4:11–12).

How quickly Jesus drew her into conversation about earthly and spiritual matters. He knew the thirst of her heart. He probably paused—giving her time to prepare for His answer. Perhaps by now, He had learned her name, and calling her by that name, He said: "Everyone who drinks of this water shall thirst again; but whoever drinks of the water that I shall give him shall never thirst; but the water that I shall give him shall become in him a well of water springing up to eternal life" (John 4:13–14).

About that time, she must have taken her water pot and put it down by the well. How significant were her actions. Perhaps she was beginning to trust this Stranger. She said: "Sir, please give me this water, so I will not be thirsty, nor come all the way here to draw" (John 4:15).

Could she have realized she was putting the empty pot down in exchange for the living, never-ending, thirst-quenching, well-springing, eternal-life water—hoping against hope that she would never have to go to that dreaded well again? She was right in asking for the living water. He was correct—she indeed would never know spiritual thirst again. Little did she realize she would never visit Jacob's well again without remembering this life-changing conversation.

. . . AND SHE WAS THIRSTY

The phone rang. I answered. It was one of my husband's choir members, asking a favor. At that time Bob was a minister of music.

The caller said that a woman from his office had just moved into the Lullwater Estates town house complex where we lived at the time. He said she really needed a friend and gave me her town house number. Because of my travel schedule, it was quite some time before I was able to knock on her door.

The opportunity finally came for me to drop by her home, and I introduced myself by saying that I was a friend of her office worker friend. We stood at the doorstep and talked. After all, why should she trust me? I'm sure we both wondered if we had anything at all in common.

Feeling a little bit awkward, I told her I traveled a great deal, but when I was at home, I tried to walk every day. At the time, we lived right next to the street where the movie *Driving Miss Daisy* was being filmed. It was a beautiful place to walk—shady, tall trees and cool breezes. I invited her into my world by asking if she would walk with me one day soon. She agreed and we followed through. After every walk, we were both thirsty and ready for a drink. As we began a journey together, I should have suspected that God would draw her to His life-giving water in me.

During the next year we walked as often as our schedules allowed, and a friendship soon developed. I learned about her family of origin, and she learned of mine. This precious woman was literally dying of thirst—thirst for the real life. She had a thirst for meaning that came from emptiness. She knew about abuse. She knew about the power of alcohol. She knew about failure and she knew about divorce. She was struggling to make some sense of life. I could feel her thirst, and I wanted to show her the way to the well. She let me know immediately she wasn't looking for a church! She said she had tried that when she was young. So . . . I became her church. She kept saying, "You seem to be so peaceful."

We opened our home to her. She was included in our evenings at the symphony. My husband is a wonderful gourmet cook, and since she also loved to cook, this became an event for us—of which I was the beneficiary! The journey to the well was up and down—two steps forward and three steps back. Like the woman at the well, she made many trips to the well just to get enough water to survive for the day.

Then the day came. She showed up at my door with a Bible in her hands, put her empty life down in front of me, and said, "I want to know the peace you have."

. . . And She Was Thirsty

On several occasions, Bob and I had watched a little red sports car and a BMW pull in and out of this beautiful home in our complex. To be honest, we wondered how a newly married couple could live in such a nice place.

Often, as I opened the front door to get the morning paper, I noticed a very well-dressed woman, briefcase in hand, step into her car and drive off. I wondered what kind of work she did. One day a quiet voice whispered: *She needs you.*

I argued with that voice, explaining my uncompleted list for that day and a busy schedule for the week—and even pretended I would do it the next week when I returned from my extended trip.

Two months later I had the same experience and, once again, rationalized with that inner voice. I was on my way to speak to a Christian women's conference to teach them how to splash the living water. (How many times have I missed an everyday opportunity to splash the living water in obedience to the Spirit of God!)

Several weeks later, I opened our front door to get the Saturday paper. My neighbor was standing there—ready to ring the doorbell. We were both surprised, and she said, "I'm looking for a man."

I said: "My man's not here! And besides I don't share, you understand." An interruption in my schedule was on its way as we both laughed. "May I help?" I asked her.

"I'm trying to get a stationary bike from my car trunk to the upstairs bedroom."

"Oh," I offered, "I can help you do that." I'd been dying to see the inside of her lovely home anyway, and this was my chance! So off we went.

Not knowing this neighbor very well, I inquired what she did, explaining that I'd seen her leave each morning with briefcase in hand. She told me that she worked in a professional office in downtown Atlanta. Then it was her turn. She had seen the taxi come to my doorstep and had seen suitcases on the doorstep very often and wondered what I did and where I went. I breathed a prayer of thanks for God's kindness at another opportunity (interruption) to share with this woman.

"I travel across the United States, speaking to and teaching women," I ventured.

"That's interesting. On what subject do you speak?"

Let me confess to you, dear reader, that I often respond to that question this way: "I speak to women about prayer and its influence in everyday living." I do this because it is an easy opener to an extended conversation. Most people know something about prayer. It worked once again.

Without asking about prayer or how I teach, she said, "Oh, would you pray for me?"

By now, I knew her name. "Janet, I'd be honored. How can I pray for you?"

Her emptiness and thirst came flooding out. "I'm a newlywed. We are quite wealthy. Well," she continued, "I *was* wealthy when I married! I did not know at the time that I had married a man who is an addictive gambler. He has lost everything I had and has now walked out on our marriage."

My heart sank. That still small voice had tried to interrupt me *six months* earlier about her need.

. . . AND SHE WAS THIRSTY

I'm a list person. Are you? I make my daily list, my weekly list, and my monthly list. I just *love* lists. I can't live without a list. My husband says that I will be miserable in eternity if I am not able to have a list. I'd love to know if you are like me. At the end of the day as I check off my list, if I've done something that day that was not on my list, I put it on—and then mark it off! I know you are laughing. I can hear it! Surely there will be a corner in heaven for all of us list makers.

Jesus also was a list maker. His list only had one thing on it: to do the will of His Father. You never see Him check things off His list because His list was His lifestyle. His whole life was a ministry of interruptions—on His way to the cross. Hebrews 12:2 says, "Fixing our eyes on Jesus, the author and perfecter of our faith, who for the joy set before Him endured the cross."

Take time to read Matthew, chapter 8. You will clearly see that on that day of His life, He was interrupted eleven times. Each interruption met the needs of the people, showed His power, and displayed God's glory. His single purpose was to be about His Father's business. On His list was the Cross. On His way to the Cross, He kept stopping along the way, embracing the interruptions, so that He could minister, heal, and offer eternal life. You might think He was collecting an army of ragamuffins, calling them to follow Him from

- Trees
- Dinner tables
- Tax offices
- Beds of prostitution

- Fishing boats
- Beds of sickness
- Hillside coliseums of thousands
- Beachside breakfast feasts
- Fish-and-bread picnics
- And . . . a Roman cross

Jesus' ministry was one of interruptions based on a heavenly agenda. Can you catch the vision of a life of interruptions . . . with a heavenly purpose? (Lord, teach me to joyfully accept Your interruptions on my list . . . Oops. I mean *Your* list.)

My life was interrupted a long time ago during a fall weekend youth retreat when I was a youth director in a local church. At the close of the campfire service, I was making my way back to my cabin when one of the young people said that Julie, one of the campers, was asking for me back at the campfire. I found her in tears and unable to talk. I waited for her to compose herself. Finally she was able to tell me that she was not a Christian. People just thought she was because of her parents' leadership roles in the church. We talked until the wee hours. When she finally prayed with me to receive Christ, I'll never forget the look of joy that veiled her face. The presence of Christ was all over her. I suggested she make her commitment known to the church family the next Sunday. She promised. That Sunday morning I prayed for the young people as many of them made their way to the altar in response to the retreat weekend.

Julie was not one of them.

Weeks passed. The youth group was full of excitement in the Wednesday night Bible study, and the interest and attendance grew and grew. I was busy with all the preparations when I finally realized that Julie was not ever there. I asked one of the teens about her absence.

"Haven't you heard? Since the retreat, she has gone back with the old crowd. She's gone back to her old lifestyle."

My heart sank. I had not been in touch with her since the retreat, and when I called to check on her she was rude and unwilling to talk to me. I struggled to think of a way to connect with her, not knowing a crisis would soon bring us together.

As I prayed asking God for direction, it came to me that I should ask her to baby-sit on Wednesday nights once in a while so my children's bedtime schedule wouldn't be continually interrupted—and it would get her back into my life. One Sunday afternoon when one of our children was ill and I needed a sitter, I called her. She answered the phone, but she said she could not come because she was too sick. She sounded terrible. I asked what was wrong, and her response was that she thought she might die. I told her I would be there in five minutes.

I left quickly, leaving my minister/husband with two small children. She met me outside her house, got in my car, and we drove around while she told a most sordid story of her young life. There was not much that she had not experienced. I offered friendship, wondering what on earth I could do to make a difference.

As I drove back home that afternoon, her words haunted me. She had said, "People in the church always say, 'Call if you need me.' You're the first one to ever come."

The journey with her lasted well over a year. It was a risk. Returning from evening activities, I found things—and some people—in my home that I would not otherwise have accepted. More prayer! More trusting the Father that He was indeed leading in this troubled relationship. The phone rang often that year, many times late in the night, and I knew it would be her, sobbing about what she had just done and wanting to know if God could forgive her. She had enormous anger at the church because she had seen firsthand un-Christlike conduct.

During that year, Bob and I wrote a youth musical called *Now Hear It Again!*, and much of the text for the musical came from my friendship with her. One of the texts said: "Are you often lonely . . .

even in a crowd?" Because I could see the depth of Julie's loneliness, these words haunted my heart. She needed someone with a listening heart whom she could trust to show her God's love.

Our fall youth revival featured a speaker from the West Coast who was having a great impact on high school students all across the Midwest. We made arrangements for him to deal with the issue of drugs at assemblies in both high schools in our city. Many people were praying that Julie would hear and respond. His message struck her so hard, she literally ran from the assembly in her high school!

I had not been asking her to come to church, but because the youth choir was to premiere our new musical, I took a risk and invited her to the opening night of the youth revival. After the musical and the message, the altar call was given. I looked everywhere for her and was disappointed, until from nowhere, she came running down the aisle and grabbed me, saying, "You wrote those words about me, didn't you?"

Through our tears, I affirmed her words, saying, "I have prayed for you to come home to the Father, and I am glad He used these words and the message to bring you home."

. . . And She Was Thirsty

An interruption? Yes! But God is looking for women who will invest their lives in children and teenagers who are in trouble, offering to them the gift of grace that is freely given to us and should be freely shared. Most teenagers need some significant adult beyond parents to help them walk the tough years of growing up. They need a coach, a teacher, a mentor, an older sister in Christ, a guidance counselor, a neighbor, or a grandmother. What an opportunity to splash the living water in your world!

One of the verses that intrigue me in my study of John 4 is verse 27: "And at this point His disciples came, and they marveled that He had been speaking with a woman." Why were they so surprised? Jesus was just being Himself, taking advantage of the interruption as He rested by the well.

Ask God to place His spirit on your interruptions, and the world will marvel at the people and places He uses to interrupt you.

During one of my seminars, a woman spoke up, and said, "After I heard you speak last year at the evangelism conference, I told my husband on the way home in the car, 'That may work for Esther Burroughs, but it sure won't work for me.'"

But then she told me this story. Her family had moved to a new community where her husband was to pastor. They quickly discovered the community was heavily inundated by one particular faith that some considered to be a cult, and the school system struggled with faith issues. She shared how she had prayed for a ministry in her children's school system. When she attended a PTA meeting, the principal asked her to consider serving on a committee to set policies. What great timing in her life.

She told the women in my seminar that she asked God for opportunities to splash, and she found them everywhere. She started a catering business part-time, and she brought food daily to a movie set in the film industry. God showed her opportunity after opportunity to splash the living water as she met physical needs with the food she had prepared each day for the actors and the production staff.

She was having a dynamic impact on the film industry by splashing the living water through her food service. She asked the seminar group to pray that God would keep her obedient and available. God splashed ordinary situations in answer to a woman's prayers.

These encounters are real! You have thirsty women in your community. Follow Jesus by looking for interruptions and realize that they can be life-giving encounters.

In my early growing-up years, my parents took in boarders to help financially. They would stay in one of the bedrooms, which meant the siblings had to share bedrooms, a common experience in those days. Most boarders would eat with our family, but if they wished, my folks provided a small hot plate for them to fix meals in their room. I don't know how, but my mother knew they were thirsty.

I do not remember this practice being disruptive to our family. It felt like extended family, in fact, and that was just what it was. What a powerful example of parenting to teach children that the home is used to splash the love of Christ. Consider using your homes for some type of personal evangelism. There are many ways to do this. I believe the lost art of hospitality is a missed opportunity to share Christ and to be an example to our children. Every missionary who came to town ate a meal in our home! I was made a global citizen before I could possibly know its impact on my life.

Bobbie Pinson, a pastor's wife, is a living example of sharing the home to splash. I heard her husband, Dr. Bill Pinson, tell about times that Bobbie used their home for evangelism. For instance, when they moved into a new neighborhood, and after they had settled, Bobbie would canvas the neighborhood, knocking on the doors of the new neighbors, introducing herself, and asking if there were children in the home. She would tell them that she was beginning a Saturday morning children's club, which included the telling of Bible stories and providing games, crafts, and refreshments, and she would like to invite their children to come and be a part of this activity—free of charge. Well, what mother in her right mind would refuse free child care on a Saturday morning? The neighbors sent the children.

. . . AND THEY WERE THIRSTY

Phyllis Harbaugh, and her pastor husband, Herb, use Halloween, a big event in their northern community, to share Christ. One year Phyllis not only gave treats to the children, but she also invited the parents into their home for hot chocolate and pop-corn. This gave her a chance to meet her neighbors and share a gospel tract in the popcorn bag. She has led many of her neighbors to Christ.

. . . THEY MUST HAVE BEEN THIRSTY

On my grandfather's farm, I remember the big salt blocks that the cattle came to in the afternoon. I watched as the cattle quietly licked the salt. Pretty soon they moved from the salt block to the watering trough, drinking in their fill of water . . . to quench their thirst.

Matthew 5:13 in *The Message* says it clearly: "Let me tell you why you are here. You're here to be salt-seasoning that brings out the God-flavors of this earth. If you lose your saltiness, how will people taste your godliness?"

In today's culture, lost in itself, you and I must live in such a way that our daily encounters develop in others a thirst to find the well of living water.

1. Have you ever been thirsty? Explain.

2. Who offered you water?

3. What is it in your life today that keeps you from heavenly interruptions and splashing the living water?

4. Make a list of potential opportunities in your neighborhood/workplace.

5. Choose one or two opportunites and put these on your prayer list and look for interruptions to share Christ. Bathe this list in prayer.

MORE SPLASHING: Study Matthew 25: 31–46.

2

ACCEPTING
THE WATER

My husband and I were on our way to San Francisco to be involved in a missions conference at Golden Gate Baptist Theological Seminary. Bob was to lead the music and I was to be the missions speaker. On our way we stopped by Vail, Colorado, to visit our son, David, who was involved in a marvelous ministry to the International World-Class Ski Championship. While there, David convinced his dad and me that we should learn to ski— and that he could teach us quickly so that we could be on the slopes in no time, sailing through the powdered snow just like the pros. I looked over the skiing crowd at Vail, and I noticed how sharp they looked in their brightly colored ski outfits! I had been an athlete in college days—I could do this! The key words in that last sentence are *had been*!

Bob and I decided to give it a try, even though I told David, "I'm not sure I can do this. I'm too old!" He, of course, stretched the truth, and said I wasn't.

What happened next should have been my first clue that skiing was not what it's cracked up to be. As we ventured out on the bunny slope, David said to us, "First, you have to learn to get up. The hardest part about skiing is learning to get up!"

I thought to myself, *That's also the hardest part about life too— just getting up after life knocks you down!*

(Or is it? Perhaps, if we, as busy, driven women, could learn to take some down time—to sit still, enjoy some quiet time, and center the heart—we would handle the getting up part of life more efficiently.)

Bob and I did quite well at first. I had fallen a few times on the bunny slope and was just getting the hang of it. Then David suggested that we take the ski lift to the next level. I'm really slow, I guess, or I would have realized what the second level meant!

For you nonskiers, you must be able to get on and get off the ski lift—at just the right moment—because other people behind you will also get off the ski lift, whether you are out of their way or not. I got off—or, it might be better to say, I fell off! I managed to quickly drag myself out of the way at just the right moment before being run over by four skis!

I got to my feet by using the skill David had taught me and moved down the ski path a bit to wait for Bob and David. I noticed how steep the mountain was—and how close I was to the edge of the ski path. I said to myself, "Get closer inside, Esther, or you'll go down the side of this mountain and make a new ski trail!" While attempting this maneuver, I fell. I don't remember if it was the pain I felt—or the sight of the glove on my right hand turned the wrong way. I cried out, "I've broken my arm!"

My words echoed across the Rockies. Bob raced to me while David went to call the ski patrol. The patrol arrived, looked at my situation, and decided to ski me down the mountain on a stretcher sled and take me to the emergency room of the local hospital. I later learned that as they skied me down the hill, I was sometimes being pulled and sometimes lifted in the air!

I can still recall two things: 1) I was wrapped tightly in the sleigh stretcher, but no one thought to take off my ski mask. I thought I might suffocate before I got down the mountain. 2) Every so often, my son, who was skiing right beside the stretcher, would lean over, look in, and say, "You're gonna make it, Mom!"

How often women desire to hear someone say those exact words, *You're gonna make it.*

Once we arrived in the emergency room, the hospital staff confirmed the break. They told me I had a clean break in the middle of my upper right arm and, in addition, I had crushed my right shoulder bone. I had done it up right. Since this kind of accident does not require surgery, they immediately placed me in a velcro wrap that held my right arm tightly in place at my waist and also sped the healing process. They put no cast on my arm.

Not only had I shattered my right arm—but I also shattered my plans for my trip to San Francisco, which was important to me. "Can I go to San Francisco—please?" I asked the doctor.

His simple reply was "No!" In fact, he sent me back to Atlanta. Bob went on to the missions conference while I returned home, in great pain and under great stress.

One of the richest times in my life developed because of a ski accident. Because of this accident, I had to cancel all my speaking engagements for about six weeks. Each day was spent in front of a fresh fire blazing in the fireplace. My Bible was in my lap, and I began reclaiming the promises God had given to me throughout my life. Many times, I had longed for and dreamed of a six-week vacation package! Who wouldn't? Like most of you, we had our children—first small, then middle school and high school age. And I had my college-professor husband, his teaching and travel schedule. And I worked outside the home as well as traveled myself. I had longed to be at home—sitting in front of the fire—reading, taking care of my heart and soul without all the responsibilities that life brings. Looking back now, I would have settled for just a day or two—not six weeks!

I had no idea that God would teach me about my worth as His daughter during those weeks. If you had asked me about my relationship to God and my freedom to be myself, I would have said, "It couldn't be better." Was I in for a big surprise!

The ski accident changed more than my arm. Spending hours in Bible study gave my life a Holy Spirit X–ray of my condition before the Father. It was as if the Father said, *Esther, I don't want your busy schedule. I want your adoration. I want the little girl in you to relax in our friendship.*

I now know there is a difference in dutifully having a quiet time and expectantly knowing the Father waits to meet me. He desires that we meet Him. I began to learn about balance—taking in and giving out, caring for body and soul, and learning to play hard and to work hard. A balance guarantees balance.

When I speak to women's groups about being a woman of God, I often deal with the issue of self-esteem. I tell them that Psalm 139 is my "horrible-no-good-very-bad-day" psalm. Look at it with me to accept your God-given designer look. The psalmist says that our Master Designer knew all about us from the time we were formed in our mother's womb, and even before we were born. He knew all the days of our individual lives. No wonder the Psalmist cries out: "I am fearfully and wonderfully made" (v.14). The Message translation of Psalm 139:15–17 says it this way:

> You know me inside and out,
> You know every bone in my body;
> You know exactly how I was made, bit by bit,
> How I was sculpted from nothing into something.
> Like an open book, You watched me grow from conception to
>   birth;
> All the stages of my life were spread out before You,
> The days of my life all prepared

Before I'd ever even lived one day.
Your thoughts—how rare, how beautiful!

He leads us to acknowledge that we can't begin to number the precious thoughts He has about us—they number more than the grains of sand. (You will never find this kind of guarantee on the designer dress label on the clothes you wear.) God says, *The life you wear* [live] *is so precious to Me, My thoughts about you are more than the sand.* Think of this promise the next time you are stuck in traffic . . . in a long grocery line . . . in your fourth car pool of the day. Put verses 5 and 17 on a card . . . and keep the card on your car sun visor. Then pull it down and bask in these words:

You have hedged me behind and before,
And laid Your hand upon me.
Such knowledge is too wonderful for me;
It is high, I cannot attain it.
How precious also are Your thoughts to me, O God!

Our culture screams to you: *Do* this! *Wear* this! *Try* this! Our heavenly Father gently whispers, *My Daughter, be still! Hush! Listen! Rest in Me. Praise Me, for you are fearfully and wonderfully made.*

Some years ago, I heard a talk-show interview with the young actor that you might remember as the TV series character Webster. The host said, "You are just like Gary Coleman. Even your shows are alike. What do you say to that?"

Webster's answer was marvelous. "No, sir," he said. "You've got that wrong, 'cause he's *he* and I's *me*."

I laughed, embarrassed in the realization that in God's kingdom, comparisons are not allowed. Women make a terrible mistake comparing. God does not have a standard by which He measures us against each other. We do that. His standard is far higher. Holy God measures each of us against His Son, Jesus. That should change your focus. God will not ask us if we wear specific clothing labels. He will want to know if we are clothed in Christ Jesus.

The biblical truth is that each woman of God is uniquely created and gifted for the purpose of bringing glory to God. This sets us apart from the world. We don't take our standard from the world's fashion designers. We take our standard from the Master Designer! He not only designs us, but He also equips us with all spiritual gifts in Christ Jesus in order to be able to live as He calls us to live!

My desire for you would be that this message be placed into your heart and life. You will never again have to look at a label in your dress as a measure of success or esteem. You will always wear God's label—Chosen in Christ Jesus—in your heart.

You can choose your Christ Esteem by choosing to accept the truth of Ephesians 1, that we are blessed in God! And what a blessing that is! Paul shows us how Jesus, the Messiah, is eternally and tirelessly bringing everything and everyone together. He has included us in this plan and chooses to work in and through us. Because we know God's plan of reconciliation, it is urgent that we accept ourselves and see ourselves as part of His plan, which is to bring the world to Himself. We must not waste time comparing our gifts, but we must use our gifts to further the kingdom. Embrace Paul's words to the Ephesian Christians as your own.

Have you ever said to someone, "Good morning, how are you?" and received the answer, "I'm blessed"? It makes you smile. Paul says we have every blessing in Christ Jesus. Our position in Christ ensures this because before He laid down the earth's foundations, He had us in mind, and chose us to be the focus of His love. Read the first chapter of Ephesians and underline each time it says *in Christ* or *in Him*. The blessings are not just for eternal life, but for life today.

I love to be around the person who lives joyfully, praising God for his every blessing. Christ chooses to bless His family. Og Mandino says, "Your life can be changed if you choose to live, in love, by four stated rules." One important rule is, Count your blessings. I tried it. As I traveled the forty-five-minute drive to work, I listed my blessings aloud. It does change your attitude. Most often I broke out in song. Your position in Christ assures that you are blessed today and forever.

Recall your engagement day. Expressing love, you were asked to share a life together. You were to be given a new name. A new direction in life. How like God to make it easy for us to understand that we are "chosen in Christ," through Him and in Him, by showing us His pleasure in His own son.

God announced at the beginning of Jesus' ministry (Matt. 3:17): "This is My beloved Son, in whom I am well-pleased." Jesus was the focus of God's delight. So are you! Don't we often find ourselves running and doing, and isn't it related to acceptance from others? Our focus is not right. It is His acceptance, which we have in our salvation, that matters. We often carry out this insecurity in the body of Christ, the very place where the whole body has acceptance in Christ. We try to prove our worth with activity—rather than rejoicing in the relationship.

I love the Scripture where God refers to us as "My people." Isaiah 43:1 says, "I have called you by name; you are Mine!" Deuteronomy 4:20 says, "But the LORD has taken you and brought you out of the iron furnace, from Egypt, to be a people for His own possession, as today." First Peter 2:9 says, "You are . . . a people for God's own possession."

Perhaps our culture's struggle with esteem is an issue of ownership. We are not our own. John 1:11 says, "He came to His own [possession], and those who were His own did not receive Him." First Corinthians 6:19–20 says, "Do you not know . . . you are not your own? For you have been bought with a price: therefore glorify God in your body."

Don't ever forget. You are His possession! We are women . . . living as cherished chosen possessions. *YES!*

Holiness is not a reward to be grasped; it is a state of becoming, a relationship to be lived. To be *holy* means to be set apart. You are set apart *by* Christ—and *for* Christ. As a bride, you are set apart for your husband, just as the church, the bride of Christ, is set apart for Christ, the bridegroom.

For too long, I thought holy living was only for Bible times or for ministers or missionaries! Perhaps I saw lives given to holiness and made the false assumption that I could not live that way, when in reality that is exactly what God calls me to do!

The prophet Isaiah prophesied Christ in chapter 35, verse 8: "And a highway will be there, a roadway. And it will be called the Highway of Holiness. The unclean will not travel on it, but it will be for him who walks that way." What way? The way of a chosen, holy one.

Matthew 7:14 refers to this same roadway: "For the gate is small, and the way is narrow that leads to life, and few are those who find it." Isn't that just like God to call His children His chosen possession and then, through the cross, make Himself a roadway inviting His chosen to become a Highway of Holiness, a walkway for others to find Christ? What an opportunity for us! Women—chosen to walk in the way of Christ.

Have you ever accused your children and had them respond, "It's not my fault! I'm not to blame!" I'm never long in my grandchildren's home before I hear someone say, "Don't blame me, I didn't do it." After a particularly hard day with her three-year-old, my daughter felt she'd been unfair with her oldest child. Waking her up the next morning, she asked Anna to forgive her.

"What for?"

"I was unkind to you yesterday, and I'm sorry."

Anna looked at her mother and said, "Forget yesterday, Mommy." *Blame* means to condemn or to be at fault. *Blameless*, then, is to be without blame or fault because someone else took all the blame.

Jesus took all the blame for our sin and cried out from the cross: It is finished . . . not guilty . . . blameless. You and I stand guilty, born in sin, and yet we need not carry the guilt. Could it be that many Christians live joyless lives because they continue to carry the blame and guilt that God has already banished from His sight? God never reminds us of what He has already forgiven.

In a recent worship service a young family was called to the altar to present their newly adopted two-year-old son. The pastor prayed a prayer of dedication, thanking God for answered prayer. The mother went back to sit with the choir. As the father took the child down the aisle, headed to the nursery, Anthony called out, "Bye, Mommy!" I cried. How quickly Anthony bonded in love with his new mother. How pleased our heavenly Father is when we cry out to our "Daddy," as adopted sons and daughters.

In biblical times, seven witnesses had to be present at adoption. The Holy Spirit is the witness of your salvation when you receive Christ as your personal Savior. The Holy Spirit is the guarantee of things to come in your life as a Christian. I'm told that you cannot undo adoption papers, and the same is true of your salvation experience. The Holy Spirit indwells you and He never leaves. Salvation is for eternity.

Think about a life that is blessed, chosen, holy, blameless, and adopted. Often teachers put stamps of approval on students' papers: GOOD, EXCELLENT. The Father's heart stamps His love for you with these words from Ephesians: "Accepted in the beloved"! Women, enjoy your position of acceptance in Christ!

Some years back we were caught up in saving green stamps, which were given by businesses where we purchased goods. We did not consider that the cost of the items we purchased might include the cost of the stamps. We filled our stamp books to purchase something free, when really we had already paid the price in the cost of groceries.

Redeemed means to pay a ransom or to buy back. Sin separated us from Christ, and He paid an awful price to buy us back. We are His by creation and because sin came into the world, God chose to bring us back to Himself through His Son's death on the cross. We are His in creation and His in redemption.

- The price was high.
- The cross was heavy.
- The debt was paid.
- The sinner is free!

We live in the shadow of the cross. How can we not accept His acceptance of us?

Women often feel we can't get it all done—can't balance family, career, church, and community. Of course we can't! But we can rely on the Father's wisdom and insight for His children. Wisdom and insight come through experiencing the journey of life. God's word promises that.

In Luke 21:15, Jesus, teaching the disciples the dangers of the life ahead of them, told them not to ever prepare to defend themselves. "For I will give you utterance [a mouth] and wisdom which none of your opponents will be able to resist or refute." James 1:5: "But if any of you lacks wisdom, let him ask of God, who gives to all men generously and without reproach, and it will be given to him."

I have two small shadow boxes in our family room. One is from the *Milligan* side of our family and the other is from the *Burroughs* side. I have hankies and wedding rings from both our grandmothers and pins from both mothers, and I have added a ring and a hankie that belonged to me. That little box contains three generations of treasures. My will states that one box is for my daughter and the other is for my son—each an heir.

Have you written your will? If you haven't, you should—immediately! Write a will so that your heirs—the ones who will inherit your estate—will know what is given to them by birthright. Do you own something that once belonged to a grandmother? Do you own something that once belonged to Christ? Yes, you do. You are joint heirs by birthright.

Your inheritance is in Christ Jesus. Whatever is His is yours. Questions for today's woman might be, Is what's yours His? Does your relationship with Christ draw you to be His totally? You are rich in Christ Jesus with a richness the world cannot possibly provide through any estate sale or will.

Everything that is given to us from our Father is to be accepted by us . . . for the purpose of giving praise and glory to the Father. We live by choosing to live in the culture, by giving praise to the Father through our lives, by acting like daughters of the King. That is true kingdom living! Don't you feel rich knowing that you are blessed . . . chosen . . . holy . . . blameless . . . adopted . . . forgiven heirs in His Kingdom?

The ski accident, mentioned earlier, taught me some valuable lessons and gave me new insight.

- What I did not want. My broken right arm caused a time of forced rest. My life literally ground to a halt! I discovered that brokenness is often a time of healing. I discovered that I was running when He was asking me to rest . . . in order to refresh, renew, and revitalize my spiritual energy. I discovered I was helping keep Delta Air Lines in business . . . and probably trying to earn acceptance when He had already offered me His acceptance.

- What I did not know. My broken right arm slowed me down and proved me almost powerless. Slowing down in anything tends to make us feel as if we are losing power. But I thought I could do it all in spite of my broken right arm! My husband literally became my right arm. He did almost everything for me during that six-week period. He was freelancing at that time and his calendar was clear, so he could be with me most of the time during the healing process. He would not only fix my meals, he would cut up the items on my plate . . . and sometimes, early in the recovery process, feed me! I learned I was completely dependent on him and had to trust him for every need.

I realized through this accident experience that humor has a valuable place in our lives. Everyone needs to laugh more! The accident changed all that. How could I not laugh at myself without makeup? I'm at the age where makeup is more important than my dress. When my husband would take the hair dryer and go one direction, and the hair brush would go in another direction, I ended up having a punk hairdo. We both laughed. I could not put on clothing by myself. I had to rely on Bob. His first attempt at putting a pair of panty hose on me could have been a video classic, to be sure. No, there are no pictures! My hose looked Technicolor from the way they were twisted. When I tried to cross my leg, the hose kept falling down. We laughed again and again.

The first time I spoke after the accident my arm was in a sling. I discovered I cannot talk without my hands. It was a terrifying experience for me. We laughed about that in the car on the way home, as he described for me that he could see and feel me losing my train of thought, needing my hands to describe my words.

I could do so little for myself. Things that once seemed so important became events for laughter. The world went right on by . . . not missing me in the slightest way. That spoke volumes to my heart. I had to laugh about all the running in my life. No one even noticed when I had to stop.

Well, God finally got my attention so I could learn intimacy . . . in quietness and with no self-sufficiency. I came before Him day after day in a childlike faith, and He whispered exactly what He wanted me to hear and understand.

The second time I spoke after the accident, a fellow staff member where I worked at that time flew back on the same plane. After hearing me speak, he gave me a good critique: "You need to use more humor in your speaking. You take yourself too seriously." He then complimented the humor I had used. That conversation became a teachable moment for me. I've been having the time of my life ever since. I had thought all along that what was important was what *you* think of me. I came to realize that what really matters is what *He* thinks of me. I now relax and let laughter come through my childlike faith.

- What I did not realize. My thirst for spiritual matters and rest before the Lord was deep. I would bask in hours of Bible study and prayer. I found myself centering internally on things spiritual and found myself thinking less and less about all my activities . . . and my future events! Time flew! I would be called to eat, thinking it was time for lunch, only to discover it was time for supper. I had rested in the Lord all day . . . and He had ministered to me through His Word, through great books, through inspirational messages and articles. I found time to visit with friends by phone and catch up on their lives. I had been too busy before the accident to even inquire about them.

One evening the dinner table was set with our best china, crystal, and silver. Bob was serving the dinner in his formal tux! He had even had flowers sent for the occasion. It was a special time, for sure! How humbling to be served and not to be able to serve in return.

I was powerless . . . and was shown that we are dependent upon each other to sustain life and thrive in community.

I am still realizing I cannot do everything by myself . . . and that I need other people in my life to help me with my journey. I am learning *He* is my only esteem.

My husband has the gift of mercy. (I don't! I've even taken a spiritual gifts test twice—trying to get it.) His gift touched me deeply and taught me the powerful work of God's love for me . . . unconditionally. God takes us at any stage and rearranges our agenda for His agenda, and He then empowers us with His Holy Spirit—doing for us what we cannot do for ourselves.

In one of my previous books, *Empowered*, I told how I was trying to get my sweatpants off at the end of a day during my recovery. Bob was kneeling down and untying my tennis shoes. I was tugging away at the sweat pants, saying to him, "I can do this by myself."

He looked up at me and gently said, "But you don't have to."

Later that evening, when we retired, he fell asleep as quickly as his head hit the pillow. Not me. Late into the night, Bob's words washed over me with the truth of God's message for me and today's woman, *But you don't have to.*

Chuck Swindoll tells the story of the time his children had a tree house in their backyard. On the door of the tree house, the children posted these rules:

- #1 Nobody act Big
- #2 Nobody act Small
- #3 Everybody act Medium

I can still hear Chuck laughing as he told it. The children were right!

Act Medium . . . or just be who you are in Christ Jesus! In Matthew 5:48, The Message translation says, "In a word, what I'm saying is, *Grow up*. You're kingdom subjects. Now live like it. Live out your God-created identity. Live generously and graciously toward others, the way God lives toward you."

1. Name the things in your life that you are trying to do all by yourself.

2. Name some ways you can begin resting in Him.

3. What are you becoming in Christ Jesus?

MORE SPLASHING: Read Anne Morrow Lindbergh's *Gifts from the Sea* (New York: Pantheon, 1991) and Richard Foster's *Simplicity* (New York: HarperCollins, 1998).

3

KEEP COMING,
KEEP DRINKING

It was my rare and wonderful privilege to read the bedtime stories to my granddaughter one night. After I finished "just one more" of Anna's stories and tucked her in, as I was leaving the room she said softly, "Nana, could you stay just long enough for me to tell you how much I love you?" I leaned back down toward her, and thought about just staying forever! She then reached up and put her little hands on my face, smiled softly, and continued, "Oh, Nana, I could never get done telling you how much I love you!"

Robert Boyd Munger states the same thought, in his wonderful little book titled, *My Heart—Christ's Home*. Munger imagines what it would be like to have Christ actually move into the home of our heart. Readers go from room to room, walking with Jesus to see what He desires in each area.

Munger first moves the reader into the family room of the heart, a quiet, warm, and comfortable room with an intimate atmosphere. Jesus likes it. It has a fireplace, sofa, overstuffed chairs, and a bookcase. Munger has Jesus speak: "Indeed, this is a delightful room. Let's come here often. I will be here every morning early. Meet Me here and we will start the day together." Morning by morning, the young man and Jesus meet together, and their relationship deepens.

After a while the young man is beginning to feel the pressures of his many responsibilities. Little by little, he begins to shorten his time with Jesus. Soon he misses one day and then another.

One morning, rushing down the steps in a hurry for an important appointment, he sees Jesus sitting by the fire. Suddenly it comes to him: "He's my guest. I invited Him into my heart! He has come as my Savior and Friend—to live with me. Yet, here I am neglecting Him." In dismay the host stops, turns, and hesitantly goes in. With downcast glance he says, "Master, I'm sorry! Have you been here every morning?"

"Yes," He says. "I told you I would be here to meet with you." The young man was even more ashamed! Jesus says to him, "The trouble is that you have been thinking of the quiet time of Bible study and prayer as a means for your own spiritual growth. This is true, but you have forgotten that this time means something to Me, also. Remember, I love you. At a great cost, I have redeemed you. I value your fellowship. Just to have you look up into My face warms My heart. So don't neglect this hour if only for My sake. Whether or not you want to be with Me, remember I want to be with you. I really love you."

I cannot tell you what an impact that story has had on my life. God Himself desires me just to look into His face. I remember those words as I come into His presence daily. He is already there when I get to my quiet time place. He can't wait to visit with me. He's anxious to hear my petitions, so we can listen together for His words. He has already prepared the lesson He will show me that day through His Word. Not only that, but He and His Father, living in me, are the empowering for my life. The Message translates Ephesians 2:21 like this: "We see it taking shape day after day—a holy temple built by God, all of us built into it, a temple in which God is quite at home."

My quiet time place draws me. When I'm on the road speaking, I miss my quiet place as much as anything in my life. I take familiar things with me to help recreate my place. Sometime back, early in the morning, I was sitting in my blue chair in my quiet place, when my husband, dressed for his workday, came down the stairs and walked over to me. He said: "I'll really miss you when you're not in that chair." A tender moment it was. His words and their meaning touched me. Friends, my husband could not miss me near as much as God misses me when I fail to meet Him each day.

Let me share a secret. Your quiet time place draws you. Then this place begins to look like you and is marked by your habits. My marks are there . . . coffee stains . . . lists . . . tears . . . crumpled Kleenex . . . ink marks . . . song notes still in the air . . . even carpet fuzz knee– and footprints. Seriously! I'm looking at those fuzz marks right now from my computer. The Message translation is right: "We see it taking shape day after day—a holy temple built by God."

Here's the rest of the secret: Eventually, *His marks are there too! And you begin to look more like Him.* Your heart begins to look like His home, and your life takes His shape as you take on the characteristics of Christ. The reason for being faithful to this relationship is simple: The soul needs nurture. In his book, *My Utmost for His Highest* Oswald Chambers asks very hard questions:

- Is the Son of God living in the Father's house—in me?
- Is the King at home in my life?

The ultimate sanctuary isn't a place. It is a person. I am the only castle in which He can live. His Kingdom in me . . . on this earth. Imagine our heavenly Father extending the life-changing invitation found in John 7: 37–38: "Jesus stood and cried out, saying, 'If any man is thirsty, let him come to Me and drink. He who believes in Me, as the Scripture said, "From his innermost being shall flow rivers of living water.""

Another invitation is Matthew 5:6. "Blessed are those who hunger and thirst for righteousness, for they shall be satisfied." This might be translated in this way: "Healthy are those who have a good appetite for God."

It would delight the Father for us to sing with the psalmist, "As the deer pants [longs] for the water brooks, so my soul pants for Thee, O God" (42:1). What an invitation—with huge eternal consequences. The verse from Matthew means, "Let him keep coming and keep drinking, keep coming, keep drinking, keep coming, keep drinking." The supply never runs out and never ends. This promise has a lifetime guarantee and is yours for the taking.

Women know about running out of everything, time . . . paper . . . patience . . . towels . . . energy . . . money. What an invitation! Life-giving water and the very presence of Christ invites you and me to partake freely. There is an underlying principle in this invitation:

Invited to *take* from *His* supply . . .

Invited to *share* from *our* supply.

As we come to Him and drink, then we can overflow and splash out to someone else. It is only as we come into His presence receiving His rich supply that you and I have anything to give. Consider the truth of 2 Corinthians 3:18: "But we all, with unveiled face beholding as in a mirror the glory of the Lord, are being transformed into the same image from glory to glory, just as from the Lord, the Spirit."

As you and I meet the Father, our lives become a mirror that reflects His love. His love reflects from Him to us and from us to others. We can always know when a woman has been in the presence of Christ. We can feel it . . . sense it . . . and, I believe, see it. She reflects Him.

John 15 is the wonderful passage that invites us to abide in

Christ as He abides in us. The study is about the relationship between the vine and the branch. When the branch is not connected to the vine, it dies from lack of nurturing. The farmer cuts it off, because it cannot possibly bear fruit with no connection. "To make a home within" is a good definition of abiding. Apart from an intimate relationship with Christ, we cannot live a Spirit-directed life.

Knowing that He wants us to look into His face so He can tell us how much He loves us is the only invitation we need to fulfill His purpose. Could it be that in knowing His love in our lives, we become His love to the world? Our culture searches through religious fads, new events, experiences, material things . . . always looking for something that will promise perfect love. We frantically seek and seek while God Himself is seeking us—just to be able to express His love to us.

All of Scripture reveals that God has always been calling His people to Himself because He is a calling God, a seeking God, a Shepherd—looking after the lambs and calling each one by name. The desire of God's heart is for His people to accept His love. Consider a few He called to Himself for His purpose:

- *God called Abraham to Himself—to father the nation.* "Go forth from your country, and from your relatives and from your father's house, to the land which I will show you; and I will make you a great nation, and I will bless you" (Gen. 12:1–2). God called with a *purpose.*

- *God called Moses to Himself—to deliver the nation.* "Therefore, come now, and I will send you . . . so that you may bring My people" (Ex. 3:10). God called with a *purpose.*

- *God called David to Himself—to shepherd the nation.* "And the Lord said [to Samuel], 'Arise, anoint him; for this is he'" (1 Sam. 16:12). God called with a *purpose.*

- *God called Esther to Himself—to save the nation.* "I will go in to the king . . . and if I perish, I perish" (Est. 4:16). God called with a *purpose.*

- *God called Peter to Himself—to build His church.* "Blessed are you, Simon Barjona, because flesh and blood did not reveal this to you, but My Father who is in heaven. And I also say to you that you are Peter, and upon this rock I will build My church; and the gates of Hades shall not overpower it" (Matt. 16:17–18). God called with a *purpose.*

- *God called Lydia to Himself—to open her home.* "And a certain woman named Lydia, from the city of Thyatira, a seller of purple fabrics, a worshiper of God, was listening; and the Lord opened her heart to respond to the things spoken by Paul" (Acts 16:14). Lydia was the first convert in Europe . . . and a woman. God called with a *purpose.*

- *God called Mary, Martha, and Lazarus—to share friendship.* "Jesus, therefore, six days before the Passover, came to Bethany where Lazarus was, whom Jesus had raised from the dead. So they made Him a supper there, and Martha was serving; but Lazarus was one of those reclining at the table with Him. Mary therefore took a pound of very costly perfume of pure nard, and anointed the feet of Jesus, and wiped His feet with her hair; and the house was filled with the fragrance of the perfume . . . 'Let her alone, in order that she may keep it for the day of My burial'" (John 12:1–3, 7). God called with a *purpose.*

- *God called Paul to Himself—to invite the outsider in.* "He is a chosen instrument of Mine, to bear My name before the Gentiles" (Acts 9:15). God called with a *purpose.*

- *God called Jesus to a cross—to offer the world a chance to look into His face and accept His love.* "God is faithful, through whom you were called into fellowship with His Son, Jesus

Christ" (1 Cor. 1:9). God will never stop calling. God calls with a *purpose.*

Let us see how we might look into His face—allowing Him to live His purpose and calling through us. If you are just beginning to take time to meet God daily, you might consider these suggestions. If you have been meeting Him for a long time, you might find refreshment or a new idea.

FIND A PLACE

For years, I thought everyone had to meet God very early in the morning, or it didn't work. I'm sure I made folks who were not morning people feel guilty. Ouch! If you are not a morning person, set a time that is right for you. I've heard my husband declare that he believes God isn't up before 6:00 A.M. It's not the time of day that is critical, but the habit. With the habit established, the time can be found. As you discipline yourself to get into the Word of God, His word will get into your life and you will come to cherish the place you meet Him.

I feel that the place itself draws you into His presence with joy and expectancy. Make this your personal sanctuary. A small corner of your favorite room will do . . . with your favorite chair. Let the place reflect you. Have a basket nearby for all your books, pens, and markers. Have a bouquet of daises, a coffee/tea mug warmer and, for sure, a throw blanket for warmth. Love the place you meet the Father. Love the Father you meet in your place.

DETERMINE A PLAN

Make a plan. Work the plan. The plan sets your purpose. Without purpose and direction, you will not accomplish your goal of intimacy with the Father, and you will become discouraged. Decide on a minimum time you can spend in your quiet place. If you have young children, your time may be only ten minutes . . . or less. That's all right. As your life stages change, and they will, this amount of time will change also. Your life and work may be such that you can't come into His presence every day. Yet some days you might find that you have more time. Don't beat yourself up about how much or how little time you can spend. But do get a plan—or it will not happen. Keep in mind you are working on a relationship . . . not an activity.

ESTABLISH A PATTERN

Every seamstress knows she must initially follow the pattern directions to complete the article she is constructing. As she improves her skill, she may be able to design the pattern herself. As you begin meeting the Father in your time of worship, consider following a pattern of worship.

PREPARE YOUR HEART

Begin by preparing your heart before the Lord. This may be no more than closing your eyes and inviting God to sit with you. I like to start with gratitude and praise. Follow this with an uplifting devotional reading or a chapter of a book. Then read the prayer requests in your prayer journal. You will always be adding requests, and you will find yourself dating answered prayers. You might then begin a Bible study. Close with a prayer time.

Try reading one psalm daily. The psalms are like hymns and prayers to our lives. Billy Graham even suggested we read one chapter of Proverbs and two psalms per day. The psalms tell us how to worship God and the proverbs tell us how to get along with people! Music is very helpful. Wonderful CDs and cassettes are available that will lead you into His presence.

READ THE BIBLE

One of the methods God uses to speak to His children is the written Word. Read the Bible devotionally as a storybook. A good study Bible will describe the setting and time of the book, and that information will help you read it as a story. Read the word of God as if you are in conversation with the Father. You will find yourself developing a thirst for God's truth.

When God's Word speaks to your heart, underline and date the passage. This will become such a joy days and months and years later as you recall His promises that have shown His faithfulness to you. I call that *walking around in the Word of God*.

MEDITATE ON THE SCRIPTURE

When my son was a little fellow, I asked him one day what he was thinking about. "About stuff," he said. As adults we need to make the time to think "about stuff." Creative brooding!

Meditate just means to think about the Scriptures. I have a friend who invites women to read the Bible expectantly. She says to read until God speaks to you in a certain verse. Then, stop to think about that verse. Pray over the verse for yourself or for someone else. You are in the company of the Lord when you meditate upon His word. In Psalm 19:14, David says, "Let the words of my mouth and the meditation of my heart be acceptable in Thy sight, O LORD, my rock and my Redeemer."

A wonderful way to meditate on God's Word is through Scripture song tapes. You can do this with your children as you carpool . . . or do the dishes . . . or even . . . iron! I recently heard a speaker say she prayed Scripture over her children's clothing as she ironed each piece. She felt her children were then covered and clothed in God's word. Keep three-by-five Scripture cards in your car or purse so you can review them in the traffic times of life.

PRAY

Dwight L. Moody said, "Every great work of God began with someone on their knees." I know of no other work that affects your work more than prayer.

Matthew 6:6 says, "But you, when you pray, go into your inner room, and when you have shut your door, pray to your Father who is in secret." Prayer is work and *prayer works*. Listen to what Oswald Chambers said about praying to God in secret: "God is in secret, and He see us from the secret place; He does not see us as other people see us, or as we see ourselves." (Aren't you glad about that?)

When we live in the secret place, it becomes impossible for us to doubt God. Get into the habit of dealing with God about everything. Chambers also says this about our prayer life: "Unless in the first waking moment of the day, you learn to fling the door back wide and let God into your life, you will work on the wrong level all day, but swing the door wide open and pray to your Father in secret, and every public thing will be stamped with the presence of God."

This is a high goal and a wonderful promise. I believe our prayer life is the most important thing in our lives. Nothing has more effect than our prayers. We must have times of closet prayer and continual prayer. Intercessory prayer depends on God's being all-knowing, all-powerful, and all-present.

When we intercede (pray in someone's behalf), we release God's power. Not long ago I was one of the speakers for a women's meeting in Illinois. I became reacquainted with a couple who had been students when Bob and I were on the faculty at Samford University, Birmingham, Alabama. They had just been assigned by a mission agency to be missionaries to an unnamed people group. No one was to know the name or location of this people group— as protection for the missionaries and their families. They asked if I would pray for them. I was delighted, and agreed to do so.

Some months later, I was the worship leader for a large conference. In keeping with the theme, flags of all the nations of the world were brought down the aisles one by one and displayed before the audience. Then black flags were presented to the congregation. The black flags represented the people of our world who have limited access to the gospel of Jesus Christ or whose countries were closed to traditional missionary service. It was a dramatic moment, indeed.

In the conference's closing service, I was sitting with my husband in the audience. The minister gave a strong call to missions. He invited the audience to consider prayer as a strategy for unreached people and language groups represented by the black flags, which were still on display. He invited the audience to come forward, receive a card and, after filling it out, commit to pray for a particular people group. He said that in the next few weeks the mission agency would send us the name of the people group to which we had been assigned. My heart wanted to respond . . . but I wanted my husband to go with me. He squeezed my hand. I figured that meant yes, so we moved into the aisle and picked up a card. We filled it out and sent it in.

The following events are indelible in my heart. Several weeks later, on a Tuesday, we received a letter from the mission agency providing us the name of the people group and information on the group for which we could pray. We immediately began to pray for this people group. I was so excited! On Thursday of the same week, I got a letter from the young couple I had met in Illinois—telling us what their situation would be, where they would live, and the name of the people group they would serve. It was the very same group the agency had given us! Yes! Yes! Who but God could orchestrate this in His kingdom work? Many things about their situation are still confidential. Prayer can access a country or language group through the power of the Holy Spirit. Women can have deep spiritual influence through prayer. Chapter 4 will center on the work of prayer in our lives and in our world.

RECORD YOUR THOUGHTS

You now have your quiet time place, you've prepared your heart, you've studied Scripture, and it's time to pray. As you meet with the Father, you will want to record what you are hearing and learning.

Many resources are available today in bookstores to assist in writing down your thoughts and prayers. An inexpensive wire-bound book will do. As you meet with God, write the Scripture verses that speak to you and record why a particular Scripture spoke to you and what it said. Stop and pray over the verse. You can even pray with your eyes open. If a verse or thought brings a member of your family or another person to your mind, pray the verse for them. Date the notation. I do this often in my Bible margin. This is a way of conversing with God. These jottings can act as your prayer journal where you record your requests and, of course, the answers. This is a wonderful record of your faith journey. You may prefer to use note cards and then file them where you can get to them as needed.

USE DEVOTIONAL/INSPIRATIONAL BOOKS

I like to keep two or three books in my place so I can pick one up and read a chapter each morning. It may be just the inspiration I need that day for the tasks ahead.

God uses the writings of people to affirm His truth in daily living. Inspirational books are a wonderful way to see the work of God. Every Christian or denominational bookstore has numerous Bible study materials, and most denominations have Bible study outlines that are available for use in personal Bible study. You will quickly discover that the writers of these books and materials are ordinary people—just like you and me—on the journey of faith. In my life, I vary devotional helps from time to time, but three things never change in my quiet time:

1. My Bible—heavily marked and tear-stained
2. *My Utmost for His Highest* by Oswald Chambers
3. A missionary prayer calendar

Oswald Chambers' *My Utmost for His Highest* calls us before God daily. My friend Henry Blackaby says about this book, "In most books, you know the author, but with Oswald, you know God." Another devotional classic is *Streams in the Desert*, by Mrs. Charles E. Cowman.

CONSISTENT BIBLE STUDY

Did you ever wonder how a Bible teacher knows so much about God's Word and why it seems so personal to her? The secret lies in her preparation to teach. She learns new truth and insight. The Holy Spirit manifests God's Word to her heart and makes it hers. She feels ownership in God's promises. That can happen for you also.

Real growth happens when you begin to study the Word of God for yourself. As you dig into the passages, perhaps assisted by commentaries and other biblical helps, you learn to depend upon God, and not upon a Bible teacher or pastor. The high privilege of personal Bible study will impact your life more than any other thing or event. And I can't think of a more exciting event than women in dynamic Bible study. Something happens when women study the Bible with other women. His Word is a love letter written to you from God. Cherish it.

HAVE A PERSONAL SPIRITUAL RETREAT

When I hear a great Bible teacher share God's Word and His blessings, it develops a thirst in my heart to know God more intimately. I've learned to mark off days for personal spiritual retreats for that very reason.

I know what you are probably thinking! *Sure, Esther! With my hectic schedule and all my responsibilities, when could I possibly have time to get away on a personal spiritual retreat?*

My answer is simply this: Make the time!

A great way to get started is to schedule a day on your calendar for this personal spiritual retreat. The ideal situation would be to get away to a nearby retreat center. Many denominations have retreat centers that can be used upon request for a small fee or love gift. When we lived in Atlanta, there was a wonderful monastery about forty-five minutes from our home. I would sneak away for a few hours, get one of their small rooms, and pray and study. It was wonderful solitude! Think about it. There is probably a beach, a park, an assembly, a lake, or even a room at your church that is near home. A place like this could be accessible to you for a few hours or a day of spiritual retreat. Take:

- Bible
- Pen or pencil
- Blank notebook
- Bible study workbook (Don't take the one you already study on a regular basis—try something brand new!)
- Light lunch or snack, if necessary

Now . . . head out for a wonderful day of quiet before the Father. I often use a day like this if I am preparing to speak to a women's meeting. I will take the program of the conference and pray over every name and event for the weekend, asking for God's anointing.

If you cannot get away for an entire day, schedule a half day, perhaps between children and work.

Or you can simply stay right in your own home. Take the phone off the hook and tell your family to leave a message on the machine because you will not be answering the phone during this time. Two uninterrupted hours can be enough for a good spiritual retreat.

Another idea might be to hide somewhere for two hours with a good book. Just the idea of getting away alone is refreshing. The "getting away" is the secret. This will take real effort; as women, we tend to see things that just have to be finished or completed. These interruptions crowd out any thought of personal retreat time, which is the very thing we need. If you can't possibly get two hours by yourself, then . . . take one hour . . . or . . . forty-five minutes . . . or a half hour! But guard the time, whatever the amount, and get started. Make a covenant with yourself . . . for yourself.

Jeremiah 2:13 is a strong word for the children of God concerning our intimacy with God. "For My people have committed two evils: they have forsaken Me, the fountain of living waters, to hew for themselves cisterns, broken cisterns, that can hold no water."

Have we through our busy schedules forsaken God—the Fountain of Living Water? When we are spiritually dry and thirsty, where do we go for refreshment? God continually invites us to keep coming and keep drinking . . . keep coming and keep drinking . . . keep coming and keep drinking . . . satisfying our spiritual thirst.

DRINKING AND SPLASHING

1. Describe your place of private meditation.

2. Does this place draw you to it? If so, how?

3. Perhaps your highest privilege is to come into God's presence. How does meeting Him impact your daily life?

4. Do the people you love know you have time with God?

5. What marks is God leaving in your life as you meet with Him daily?

MORE SPLASHING: Study John 15:1–16 and do the following:
- Find the meaning of the word *abide*.
- Underline each time the chapter says *abide in*.
- Tell how abiding is related to bearing fruit.
- Memorize verse 16.

4

INTIMACY
THROUGH PRAYER

It was early morning in the fall of 1944. I quietly left my bedroom, crossing the hallway to the bathroom to begin making my preparations for the day. I heard his familiar voice. *Who could he be talking to this early in the morning?* An inquisitive child, I followed the sound of his voice. The door stood slightly ajar, and I carefully peeked inside. I have carried this Kodak moment all of my life. My preacher-daddy was on his knees, his Bible open on his chair, and he was tenderly praying a psalm back to God. I felt a hushed presence. I could tell my daddy knew to whom he was talking, he was so intimately acquainted with his heavenly Father.

Even when I was a child I wanted to know God like that. I stood there hoping that presence would come to me. In the ensuing years I have discovered I can know God like that—by daily meeting God like that. By example my precious daddy taught me to practice the presence of Christ. Prayer is a conversation that never ends. That should thrill women, because we are relational and because in this conversation the listener and the friend never stop listening.

In my family of origin, my siblings and I quietly laughed when we talked about prayer and our mother. "If you need prayer, call Neva. She has a direct line to God." The real truth is, each one of us has a direct line to God because of the cross.

On my life journey, I have been privileged to meet friends who are real prayer warriors. Thelma Bagby, a missionary retired after serving thirty-five years in Brazil, chose to pray for me. This was indeed a woman of prayer. When she prayed, heaven seemed to stand still. Not only did she pray for me, but when I got back home from a speaking engagement she would also call and ask what had happened at the meeting!

She called me to accountability after every engagement. She would say something like this over the phone: "Where were you on March 25? I must know! What did God do? I was not released from my knees that morning on your behalf until noon. God must have done something awesome."

I would have to check my calendar to remember where I was speaking. And more than once I've cried before God at His power and glory, which was displayed because of the power of Thelma's prayer life in my behalf and in behalf of that particular meeting. What an awesome privilege—to be prayed for and to know God answers these prayers, just because an obedient child has prayed. We became pen pals. When the mail would bring a letter with her familiar penmanship, I would tear it open expectantly. She would speak immediately of kingdom business with little salutation. Often her letters were about her latest conversations with God, and almost always there was a word for me from that conversation.

I have introduced you to Thelma Bagby because in our correspondence through the years we have shared our thoughts on prayer with each other. Now I would like to share some of these with you.

PRAYER IS THE FIRST STEP TO KNOWING JESUS

It was Saturday night. All was finally quiet when I looked up to see our seven-year-old daughter, Melody, enter the room. By the look on her face, I could tell she wanted more than another drink of water or some other ploy to stay up just a little longer. She crawled into my lap, put her arms around my neck, and said these words: "Mommy, I love Jesus and I want to ask Him into my heart." Those words are a privilege to hear, a privilege to which every parent should look forward. I'd prayed the day would come. I got my Bible and began sharing the Scriptures with her. I cried for joy as she repeated the words of confession and invitation for Jesus to come into her heart. We will always remember that next Easter service as our pastor, Dr. Peter James Flamming, said these wonderful words: "I baptize you, my little sister, in the name of the Father, the Son, and the Holy Spirit."

That first step in knowing Jesus is a childlike prayer of confession. What a high privilege and responsibility it is for parents to lead their children to Christ. The home—even more than the church—gives spiritual instruction. Perhaps the first lesson children learn in faith is to trust their heavenly Father in prayer.

That night as I shared a simple gospel with Melody, I was transported back to my own childhood experience in accepting Christ in my heart. I share my birthday with a twin brother. He is six and a half hours older than I am! Yes—six and a half hours! That was back in the dark ages and the doctor did not even know my mother was expecting twins! I am so glad they found me, because God had a plan for my life.

As a preacher's child I was raised in a family that observed the Sabbath. On Saturday, my mother made all the preparations, which included shoes being shined . . . clothes being made ready . . . and, of course, taking Saturday-night baths. (I still cherish my heritage of Sabbath rituals.) The rule in our home was simple: if you misbehaved in church, you got spanked after church. With five children and no nurseries, one or more of us got *it* every Sunday. I was almost an adult before I realized that a spanking was not part of the order of worship in a Baptist church!

I was raised in a time when children had *Sunday* clothes and *school* clothes. When our Sunday clothes were too small, then, and only then, did they become school clothes. I remember the day I asked Jesus into my heart.

It was a Saturday morning. My older sister, Moyra, came into the kitchen, dressed up in her Sunday clothes. Mother said: "Moyra, what are you doing dressed like that?"

"I'm going over to Daddy's study. I'm dressed up today because I'm going to ask Jesus into my heart." Off Moyra went to the church. That was all it took.

I also had been feeling the tug of God's love in my life but had not been brave enough to respond. I knew in my heart I wanted to belong to God's family. When Moyra was out the door, I hurried upstairs, changed from my play clothes into my Sunday clothes and was almost out the front door on my way to Daddy's study when my mother stopped me cold and asked where I was going. I responded much like my sister: "I want to ask Jesus into my heart too." I was sent back upstairs and instructed to get back into my play clothes!

I was really ticked off, but that was before I knew you could be mad at your mother! I'm sure that in my mother's life experience, she thought I was just copying my sister. I prayed as I changed into my play clothing. "God, hurry and let Sunday get here."

I was the first to arrive in my Sunday school class that morning. As soon as my teacher, Marjorie Gordon, came into the room, I asked her to tell me how I could get Jesus into my heart so I could be in God's family. She opened her Bible and showed me John 3:16. She led me to read the verse, putting my name in place of "whosoever". I knelt on that cement floor by a little wooden chair and asked God to take away my sin and come into my heart. I could not wait to get home after church so I could announce to my family that I belonged to God's family too. I knew so little of what it would come to mean to me. I knew enough, though, to excitedly tell my family and friends about being in God's family.

Prayer is the first step to knowing Jesus. And it is always a conversation between a child and a Father.

PRAYER IS THE CONVERSATION BETWEEN A CHILD AND A FATHER

When our daughter, Melody, was eighteen months old, it was a nightly bedtime ritual and my pleasure to help her say her bedtime prayers. One evening I asked her if she would like to speak to God. "Yes," she said, bowing her head. She prayed, "Hi, God!"

My heart was touched, and I'm sure, so was the heart of God. Jesus Himself called His Father *Daddy*. I'm grateful for this model of intimacy.

To embrace the truth of Romans 8:34 is to understand prayer: "Christ Jesus is He who died, yes, rather who was raised, who is at the right hand of God, who also intercedes for us." Get the word picture that is painted here! Jesus stands at God's right hand . . . with His hands stretched toward us, receiving our prayers, and handing them to God, our Father. That is a guaranteed promise.

If that is not enough for you, read Romans 8:26: "The Spirit also helps our weakness; for we do not know how to pray as we should, but the Spirit Himself intercedes for us with groanings too deep for words."

How often as a child of God I could not get the words past my broken heart, so I just cried and Jesus explained the reason to God. I can hear Him say, *It's Esther again, and her tears are for* . . . Our Father invites us to pray. In Jesus' life, He modeled prayer for us—like a child and a father having ongoing conversations.

It used to be my habit as an adult child to call my parents every

Sunday afternoon to check on them and see what was going on in their lives. It was also a good opportunity to share prayer requests. My burden somehow felt lighter after sharing it with my parents. I knew full well that they would pray for me. We have the same privilege with our heavenly Father. Jesus stands at the right hand of God, waiting for our requests. He gives us permission to make the desires of our hearts known to Him. He invites us into conversation with Him. In a good conversation, there is both talking and listening.

Prayer is a conversation between a child and a father. And prayer is a table for two: you and God.

PRAYER IS A TABLE FOR TWO—YOU AND GOD

"You are hereby invited to . . ." The dinner invitation has been extended and you can't wait to get there. You are seated around the table with other special guests. You feel honored and can't wait to tell your best friend who sat next to you at the table. Perhaps you even want to share part of the conversation with her.

Yet God Himself, through Jesus, invites you to *His* table. Acts 2:42 says, "And they were continually devoting themselves to the apostles' teaching and to fellowship, to the breaking of bread and to prayer." This is a table—just for two. How intimate. A time to be cherished. I wonder how often He sits at the table, waiting for His invited guests to come. Martin Luther said: "As it is the business of the tailor to make clothes, the cobbler to mend shoes, so it is the business of Christians . . . to pray." Perhaps your time of prayer would have more meaning if you envision a table for two, a quiet place for intimate conversation. Like the church at Pentecost, we are called to continually break bread with the Master and to pray. E. M. Bounds, author of five books on prayer, says: "We should view prayer as constant fellowship, an unbroken audience with the King. We must see the expectation to pray not only as a divine summons but also as a royal invitation to the throne. We have the privilege of an audience with the King of kings."

Growing up in Canada, we celebrated May Day. I was in grade school when Princess Elizabeth (now Queen Elizabeth) visited our city. In preparation the teachers instructed the girls how to curtsy before the princess and how to behave in the presence of royalty.

If I were invited today to visit Queen Elizabeth, I would certainly make all the correct preparations. I would even have someone do my hair and help me select my dress. When I arrived in London to see her, I would not rush into the castle and into her court yelling, *Hello!* (or *Help!*)

Think about it. We do that all the time in the presence of the King of kings. Yes, the King is there to help us, but He also longs for our hearts to come into His courts, acknowledging His Majesty with praise and adoration.

Jesus expects us to pray. Matthew 6:5 says: "And when you pray"; Matthew 6:6 says: "But . . . when you pray"; Matthew 6:9 says: "Pray, then, in this way"; and Luke 11:9 says: "And I say to you, ask . . . seek . . . knock." Hear that as the King's invitation. The table is set. The honored guest is always present. He waits for the child to sit down at the table. Never be hurried out of your prayer time.

Prayer is a table for two—you and God. And prayer is giving God access to your needs.

PRAYER IS GIVING GOD ACCESS TO YOUR NEEDS

Your prayer life reveals what you believe about God. Jeremiah 33:2–3 speaks about the restoration of God's people: "Thus says the LORD who made the earth, the LORD who formed it to establish it, the LORD is His name, 'Call to Me, and I will answer you, and I will tell you great and mighty things, which you do not know.'"

John 14:12–14 invites you to use His name when you pray: "Truly, truly I say to you, he who believes in Me, the works that I do shall he do also; and greater works than these shall he do; because I go to the Father. And whatever you ask in My name, that will I do, that the Father may be glorified in the Son. If you ask Me anything in My name, I will do it." He has given you His name. Use it in prayer!

My mother was a woman of prayer. Nothing in her life was too big or too little for God. I can remember thinking that my mother could take a nickel and pray that it would have the value of a dime. She was a women of strong resolve, telling God her every need. And she was a woman of simple, childlike faith. When she prayed, she expected God to work. She took God at His word, often quoting Scripture to Him. Simply acting out her faith, she prayed. She told me she prayed while she ironed. Imagine wearing clothes that have been covered in prayer. What great covering!

After two hard years, my mother died of Alzheimer's disease in the summer of 1996. Following the service, my father asked me if I would like to have her prayer journals. I was so pleased. I had seen my mother keep these dime-store coil notebooks with her Bible. It felt invasive and yet empowering when I saw her commitment to letting God know her needs. It took months before my heart was ready to read her prayer journals. Finally, during the week between Christmas and New Year's Day, I took the time to do so. It was a humbling and inspirational experience.

I found my name many times as our family moved, sold homes, had grandchildren, experienced college and travel . . . every little thing that life brings. I saw the names of my brothers and sisters and the issues that related to their lives. Grandchildren problems were all taken to the Father daily. She prayed for the church family, for neighbors, for friends, for financial and medical issues, for her own needs. I found the names of some of those boarders who stayed with us—dated where she prayed for their salvation and dated again when and if they came to know Christ.

Mother listed her prayer requests on the left side of the page.

On the right side she dated the answered requests—I could tell because the ink color was different. In the later stages of her deadly disease, she was still making entries in her prayer journal. The journal must have been a place of safety for her when death was cruelly taking her life. I was overwhelmed when I realized that on many pages, she listed the request on the left side and just wrote *thank you, thank you* by each request on the right side . . . in the expectancy that the Father would answer her requests. What a walk of faith she lived! I learned from my parents to pray specifically, not generally.

Prayer is giving God access to your needs. And prayer releases the power of God.

PRAYER RELEASES THE POWER OF GOD

I was speaking at a women's meeting in Oklahoma. I often talk about my children, as most women do. I shared how we had prayed for some twenty years for the mates God would provide them. Our son met and married a young woman who had been born and raised in southern Africa by missionary parents. I was telling the audience that day how grateful I was that God had led our son to Colleen and how grateful I was for her parents and for the community of missionaries who helped raise her. I said, "All these years as I have daily prayed for missionaries and their children, I had no idea that God was preparing Colleen for David." The women warmed to my words, because every mother is concerned for the marriages of her children. My intent in the story was to remind the women to pray for their missionaries and then to realize the awesome truth that when we pray, God's power is released to do His work.

What I did not know was that there was a missionary present in the audience from southern and eastern Africa! After the meeting, this missionary, Barbara, came to me and handed me a child's blanket. She said, "As children, Colleen and my son were very good friends." She continued, laughing. "I picked Colleen for my daughter-in-law, but since you won, I brought you Colleen's 'blankie' that she gave my son as she boarded a plane to furlough in the U.S." What a thrill for me—to meet one of the women who had loved and helped raise Colleen on the mission field. I was looking into the face of an answered prayer. That's awesome! Women, when we pray, God's power is released.

Second Corinthians 1:20 says, "For as many as may be the promises of God, in Him they are yes." We pray knowing God's faithfulness through His promises in the Word.

Proof of this Scripture goes on and on . . . I heard Dr. Helen Rosevere tell this story from her experience in the Inland Mission in Zaire, Africa. Dr. Rosevere was called out in the middle of the night to deliver a baby, a preemie. But the mother did not live. The doctor asked a helper to bring a hot water bottle for this little one. She returned and told the doctor that when she put the hot water in the bottle, it burst. The helper was then asked to keep the baby warm with her own body during the night.

The next day in her prayer time, Dr. Rosevere told the children about the premature baby and the mother. Nammy, a ten-year-old African child, said, "Let's pray that God will send us a hot water bottle."

Helen thought to herself, *I know how to have faith like that, but how could I? We are in the Congo of Africa and who would think to send us a hot water bottle!*

Nammy prayed this prayer: "God, send hot water bottle today. Tomorrow will be too late. We need it today. And while you are at it, God, send a dolly for the baby's sister so she will know you still love her."

Later that day, a runner came to Dr. Rosevere's office to tell her that a car was at her home. She ran quickly, only to discover the car had already gone—but a box had been left on her doorstep. She gathered the children since this was a special occasion. The children jumped for joy when Dr. Rosevere pulled a brightly colored vest from the big box. They loved the candy she pulled out next, but they were not excited about the bars of soap.

Then Nammy rushed forth and began to tear into the box with Dr. Rosevere. She pulled out a hot water bottle! She said, "If He sent this, there must be a doll!" Further digging did indeed bring forth a doll.

I tell this story often, and each time my heart bows before God in His extravagant love toward us. Who but God could have orchestrated those circumstances?

Six months earlier, a Women's Mission Society, in London, England, had prayed for the missionary, Dr. Rosevere, and were led to send her a box that included a hot water bottle and a dolly. Imagine that! Women on one continent praying and sending supplies and becoming God's answer for another continent—six months ahead of schedule. That, my friends, is the mighty handiwork of God! Only eternity will reveal the faithful prayers of God's people and how through them God's power was released to change eternity.

Prayer releases the power of God to work. And prayer is the soul on its knees.

PRAYER IS THE SOUL ON ITS KNEES

Ephesians 6:18 reads: "With all prayer and petition pray at all times in the Spirit." Talking to men for God is a great thing, but talking to God for men is greater still. Someone has said, "Praying without ceasing is praying with the frequency of a hacking cough."

The story is told of a young man visiting in England in the home of the great preacher, A. B. Simpson. The guest was on his way out the door for an early morning walk. Going down the hallway, he passed Dr. Simpson's room and saw the minister in his study at his desk. He stopped to politely greet him when he realized the minister was reading God's Word. About to say good morning, he watched quietly as Dr. Simpson closed his Bible and reached over to take a globe in his hands.

The great missionary preacher began to pray. The young guest stood still as if on holy ground. He listened and watched as the pastor held the globe close to his chest and began to pray for the world. As he prayed, tears began to flow and roll down over the nations of the world. The guest stood still in the presence of a soul on its knees before God. Jim Elliot, the martyr who died as a missionary in Ecuador, said: "God is on the throne . . . we are on His footstool . . . only a knee's worth away."

Prayer is the soul on its knees. And prayer is serving on an executive committee for world evangelism.

Prayer Is Serving on an Executive Committee for World Evangelism

While working with a national mission agency, I was invited to speak to a women's mission group in North Carolina. I did not have Nona Bickerstaff's name on my note page and had not even planned on telling her New York City missionary story, but it must have been in my heart, because the story rolled from my heart as I told of her request to the mission agency for funds to be able to extend the two-year term of a college student for another year.

The student said, "If the funds were rejected due to other pressing needs, I will stay anyway, because God called me and the need is so great." Living with little or nothing, she continued to serve. It would only take three thousand dollars to keep the student on the field.

I said to my audience, "How can you and I not give generously to help meet the needs of one who so generously serves in the inner city?"

After my message I took my seat on the front row. As the *amen* was said, I heard a commotion in the choir loft where the officers of the organization were seated, having just been installed. They were joyfully crying, and celebration was evident. It was not long till the president of the organization, followed by all the officers, circled me and spoke words so quickly and so full of emotion I could barely understand them. Finally I heard, "We produced and sold a cookbook—and we put the three thousand dollars we made in sales in savings, and we have been arguing over what to do with the money for three years. Now we know." She wrote me a check right on the spot. I hand delivered it to the president of the mission agency.

Prayer is serving on an executive committee for world evangelization. And prayer is an audience of One.

Prayer Is an Audience of One

I was invited to speak to a church on a Sunday morning. My husband was to lead the music in that service. As we made our way to the platform, the minister said to us, "There is a woman from Russia in our congregation. She worships a little differently from our congregation, and we are not sure what to do with her."

With that information, he left to take his seat across the platform. As my minister/husband stood and invited the congregation to sing, it was not long till I saw the woman from Russia. She stood with the congregation, not dressed in bright and rich colors as others near her. She appeared to be dressed in black. She had on a long overcoat, boots, and a babushka covering all but her face. I saw her hands and voice lifted singing, "Alleluia." I knew that word—the same in most languages.

Later in the service, the minister asked the family of God to bow in prayer. I prayed with my eyes open and watched for my sister from Russia. She stood up, moved out into the aisle, got on her knees, and moved to the altar praying, "Alleluia." My heart wept for courage to get on my knees and crawl to the altar to pray. I was not sure I could speak that morning after her sermon to my life. I did my best.

The offering was taken at the close of worship. Once again I was called to bow before Holy God as I watched this woman stand and reach deep into the pocket of her coat and pull out a hankie. She untied the knot and emptied the contents into the offering plate. My heart observed, *Prayer is an audience of One.*

Prayer is heaven touching earth. We come week after week to worship in freedom. How is it possible that in worship we are so close to His presence . . . yet so far from His power? Could it be our inability to bow?

My childhood Kodak moment of my father praying was etched in my heart again many years later in a different place and a different time. On a visit in the home of my parents who lived at that time in East Texas, we were watching the Winter Olympic games in Calgary, Canada, and enjoying the beautiful ice skating events. When the American skater, Debbie Thomas, did not win the gold medal, my father got up, said his good night to us, and made his way to his bedroom. My mother and I stayed until the very end of the skating competition—hoping against hope that the results might change and that Debbie Thomas might be declared winner by default. Finally giving up, I made my way down the hall to the guest room. Passing my parent's bedroom room, I saw my father . . . on his knees at the end of the day, praying to his heavenly Father. I cried within myself, *O God, let my children see me on my knees before You.* I do not desire that my children and grandchildren necessarily see me on my knees for the show but for the picture that could be ingrained in their minds. I do desire that I live in such a way that they sense that I daily bow before God—just as my father does.

Prayer is an audience of One. Women of God—pray!

PRAYING AND SPLASHING

1. Write when and where you prayed to know Jesus and to give your heart to Him.

2. Answer this question: Do you talk more *about* God than *to* God?

3. Read Matthew 6:5–6 and describe an answer to a prayer you prayed.

4. Which statement best describes your prayer life? Why?

 Prayer is the first step to knowing Jesus.
 Prayer is the conversation of a child and a Father.
 Prayer is a table for two—you and God.
 Payer is giving God access to your needs.
 Prayer releases the power of God.
 Prayer is the soul on its knees.
 Prayer is serving on an executive committee for world evangelism.
 Prayer is an audience of One.

MORE SPLASHING: Read Richard Foster's *Prayer: Finding the Heart's True Home* (San Francisco: Harper, 1992).

5

CLOTHED IN
THE SPIRIT

After a particularly tiring week, and with many of the children still around her, Mildred McWhorter, a missionary in the inner city of Houston, Texas, was finally saying good-bye for the day. The little boy she was holding in her arms looked up into her eyes, and said: "Miss 'Quater, are you God?"

She drew back in surprise as she continued to hold him and said, "Oh, no, I'm not God . . . but God's love lives in my heart."

"No!" the little guy insisted, "You are God!"

Taking another deep breath, she said, "Oh, no! I am not God, but His Son, Jesus, lives in my heart."

As he pointed to her heart, the little boy insisted again, "Oh, no. I can see Him right there."

Imagine living in the power of the Holy Spirit so clearly that a child feels he can see God in your life!

After working twenty-nine years in the inner city, Mildred McWhorter finally retired. But the city of Houston would be forever changed! Mildred won almost every humanitarian award that could be given by that city, but none of the awards mattered to this missionary giant. She chose to live in the inner city—with the people with whom and to whom she had ministered all those years.

Paul says in 2 Corinthians 3:1–5:

> Are we beginning to commend ourselves again? Or do we
> need, as some, letters of commendation to you or from you? You
> are our letter, written in our hearts, known and read by all men;
> being manifested that you are a letter of Christ, cared for by us,
> written not with ink, but with the Spirit of the living God, not
> on tablets of stone, but on tablets of human hearts. And such
> confidence we have through Christ toward God. Not that we are
> adequate in ourselves to consider anything as coming from our-
> selves, but our adequacy is from God.

I'd like to live like that, wouldn't you . . . a letter from Christ, written by the Spirit of the living God, on tablets of human hearts.

I was attending a conference in Hawaii several years ago and was in a Bible study on Gideon defeating the Midianite army. When the teacher got to Judges 6:34, my eyes stayed glued on the page. It read, "So the Spirit of the LORD came upon Gideon; and he blew a trumpet, and the Abiezrites were called together to follow him." I looked in the margin for a reference dealing with the words, *came upon Gideon*, and found that it meant "clothed." The most amazing thing about the Word of God is its freshness in our lives. I am sure I had read that text before, but that day it was as if the Holy Spirit had highlighted it with a yellow marker. I remember putting a stickie on the page to remind me to look it up when I got home. A truth about the Holy Spirit is that He indwells you, clothes you in His power, and chooses to go before you as He is working ahead of you.

After that trip, I began looking at the work of the Holy Spirit in the Bible. I read books about the work of the Holy Spirit. I was drawn to this study and understood the reason why about six months later when a mission agency invited me to write a book about the work of the Holy Spirit in the lives of ordinary people. The Spirit had already begun to teach me about Himself.

I really loved the concept and thought of the Holy Spirit clothing me. I was so excited because I know about women—and clothes. I knew women would get this concept quickly! Imagine being dressed in the Holy Spirit! What a clear word picture for us to remember. Just as we dress ourselves appropriately for the day's activities, imagine the Holy Spirit dressing us for the activity He plans for our lives on any given day. We must remember the Holy Spirit is a Person. The Bible refers to the Holy Spirit as the Teacher, the Guide, the One who comes along beside us.

God is committed to the task of working in us, developing us, and deepening the character traits of His Son in us through the Holy Spirit until we look like Him. We are not on our own in this process. He has given us the person of the Holy Spirit to see that we become like Him in every way. In fact, the gift of the Holy Spirit was given to us the moment we accepted Him as our personal Savior. The question the little boy asked Mildred McWhorter was thought-provoking. You see, he had seen the reflection of Christ in Miss 'Quater, as he called her, and he sensed the Spirit of God in her—knowing she was a living letter.

What a great witness! When I think of Mildred McWhorter, I think of a woman full of faith and the power of the Holy Spirit. Ephesians 5:18 says, "Be filled with the Spirit." That literally translates, "Be being filled." The great preacher Dwight L. Moody is reported to have said, "We need the continuous filling of the Holy Spirit—because we leak!"

In Ephesians 1:13, we read these words:

> And you also were included in Christ when you heard the word of truth, the gospel of your salvation. Having believed, you were marked in him with a seal, the promised Holy Spirit, who is

a deposit guaranteeing our inheritance until the redemption of those who are God's possession—to the praise of his glory (NIV).

We should be as intimately acquainted with the person of the Holy Spirit as the disciples were acquainted with Jesus. Everywhere they went with Him, they felt and experienced His presence. As you and I live out our daily lives, we do so with the presence of the Holy Spirit indwelling us. The doctrine of the Trinity is having faith in the work of the Triune God: God the Father . . . God the Son . . . and God the Holy Spirit. I cannot explain the three-in-one and one-in-three concept of Holy God. Neither can I explain that water can be ice and steam as well as liquid. But I do know I need water in all three forms at different times . . . ice, steam, and water. I accept that water can also be ice and steam. God the Father . . . sent God the Son . . . and God the Son . . . sent God the Spirit. I believe that today's Christians must be intimately acquainted with the third person of the Trinity, the Holy Spirit.

Teaching about the Holy Spirit, I said to an audience on the West Coast, "If you only trust the work of God the Father and God the Son, you only have two-thirds of the power." An older woman responded, "Oh, no. You ain't got *no* power!" I stood well corrected that day.

THE PERSON OF THE HOLY SPIRIT

Growing up in church I heard messages about the Holy Ghost. My child's mind conjured up images that I couldn't imagine had anything to do with God, and I was sure I wasn't supposed to believe in ghosts. I was an adult before realizing through study that the Holy Spirit is a person, the third person of the Trinity. For you and me to know the reality of the Spirit in our lives, we must look at the person, the presence, the authority, and the filling of the Holy Spirit, enabling us to acknowledge and embrace the power of Holy Spirit.

When Jesus lived on earth, He ministered through His physical presence. He ministered in places He could reach physically. The person of the Holy Spirit does not have a physical body and is thus free to minister wherever He chooses. But the Holy Spirit is a person . . . the third person of the Trinity. You have felt His presence many times. Don't you often walk out of worship saying to yourself, "Wow! We could really feel the Holy Spirit this morning!"

In your own time of worship, the wind of the Spirit will often draw you through the refreshment of His Word. I think of the Spirit in terms of the breath of God. The old hymn sings, "Breathe on me, Breath of God, until my heart is pure." Amy Grant sings a wonderful Christmas song as a prayer of Mary. The song pleads, "Breath of heaven, pour over me Your holiness, for You are holy." This could be your moment-by-moment prayer for the breath of the Spirit to pour over—and through—you.

One of the Bible terms for the Holy Spirit is *wind*. In speaking of the new birth, Jesus says to Nicodemus in John 3:8, "The wind blows where it wishes and you hear the sound of it, but do not know where it comes from and where it is going; so is everyone who is born of the Spirit."

The Holy Spirit is the sent one. We do not need to cry for the heavenly Dove to come among us. The Holy Spirit is already among us! The Holy Spirit is here—now. We did not ask for the Holy Spirit. He is the sent one. Listen to what Jesus said about the Holy Spirit: "But I tell you the truth, it is to your advantage that I go away; for if I do not go away, the Helper [the one called alongside to help] shall not come to you; but if I go, I will send Him to you" (John 16:7).

God sent the Spirit—a member of the Godhead—to work through us. It is through the ministry of the Holy Spirit that every other ministry of God becomes real to us. The Spirit adopts us into the family. He regenerates us and cleanses our lives. He indwells us so we embrace the whole of the Trinity: the Father, the Son, and the Holy Spirit. He teaches us, speaking through His Word. He reveals to us the things of Christ that we cannot see, and this enables us to glorify God. He empowers us by personal relationship, pouring out His power through us.

THE WORK OF THE HOLY SPIRIT

When you and I think about a doctor, we immediately know the role that he has. He relates to health issues, medicine, medical knowledge, hospitals, emergency rooms, surgery, birth, death, and more. Medically trained, he is charged with administering his medical gift. His work embraces all phases of medicine, but not all at the same time. So we may see him in different settings and circumstances, using different parts of his gift, as he practices medicine.

The person of the Holy Spirit also has different roles. He is teacher, guide, power, truth, helper, and gift giver, to name some. One work of the Spirit is to draw persons to Himself.

In Acts 10:1–5, we read the story of Cornelius and his vision, which tells him to go to Joppa and bring back a man called Peter. Did you ever wonder why the angel did not tell Cornelius how to be saved? The angel instead said to go get Peter. The angel did not tell him because the angel could not tell him. The angel did not know salvation. God had to use an instrument that knew salvation. Peter was to be that instrument.

Cornelius sent two of his servants and one of his soldiers to get Peter. About noon the following day, as they were on their journey, Peter went up to the roof to pray, and he had a vision about eating meat that was unclean. While Peter was still thinking about the vision, the men sent by Cornelius found Peter's house and called out to him. Peter was still thinking about the vision when the Spirit said to him, "Simon, three men are looking for you. So get up and go downstairs. Do not hesitate to go with them, for I have sent them" (Acts 10:19–20, NIV).

How clear it must have been both to Cornelius and Peter that the Spirit preceded them in that the Spirit spoke to both of them because they were both obedient to the message. And because of this, the Gentiles heard the gospel. I believe the Holy Spirit speaks as clearly and as specifically in our lives. Trust the Holy Spirit to be just that. In your quiet time or in worship, has a thought nudged you and your mind replied with the thought, *I can't possibly do that—not now anyway.* Or, *What would people think or say, if I were obedient to the Spirit's voice?* Pause to reflect to whom you are answering. It is the whisper of the Spirit.

A woman in one of my recent seminars told about her friendship with a couple in her church and her prayers that they might come to know Christ. The wife responded first. Then she and Penny continued for a long time to pray for the husband, Jim. Both continued to ask him if he was ready. His response was always the same: "I'm just not ready quite yet."

Some months later in a special service, the couple was in attendance. Penny said that during the invitation, the Holy Spirit whispered to her to go and stand by Jim and simply say, "Are you ready yet?" He was ready . . . and he did accept Christ. His response to her afterward was this, "I was just praying, 'God, let Penny come back and get me and take me to the pastor. I'm ready.'" Wow! Trust that the Holy Spirit's work is to precede your work.

One could wonder at the results of the work of the Holy Spirit if Christians were immediately obedient to the Spirit's voice. We second-guess, pondering where that thought came from—instead of in faith, obeying the whisper of God's Holy Spirit.

It is so freeing to me as a child of God to know that I am not responsible for leading someone to Christ! What a joy to discover I am not in charge of conviction of sin. That is the work of the Holy Spirit. We make this splashing much too difficult on ourselves.

- Splashing is not about a program.
- Splashing is not about a memorized presentation.

SPLASH THE LIVING WATER

- Splashing is not about doing something.
- Splashing is not about passing or failing.
- Splashing is about relationships.
- Splashing is about friendship.
- Splashing is about the real self.
- Splashing is about being the fragrance of Christ.

As my dear friend the late Thelma Bagby would say, "It's about two people—in love . . . God and you!"

We are in a relationship with Christ, and talking about that relationship should be the most natural thing to do. I believe women sometimes fear sharing Christ because we may have the mistaken view that *we* are responsible to win that person to Christ. The good news is this: winning that person to Christ is the Holy Spirit's work! That is the work He came to do. It is not ours, and we can relax in that fact. Our work is to be obedient to share Christ in the naturalness of who we are . . . with the gifts we have been given. We can tell our story and share our relationship with another person, but *we* cannot save them. That is the work of the Holy Spirit.

I was to be in Richmond, Virginia, for several days speaking for several different events. I lived in Atlanta, Georgia, at that time and thought of the state of Virginia as the North, so I assumed the weather would be cold. It was not! In fact, there was a heat wave—in early March. My room was on the front side of the hotel, and the sun's heat poured through the window. I had walked early that morning—not wanting to walk in the hot sun. After a good shower, my body was ready for that first cup of coffee to enjoy in my quiet time. My mind said, *No! Iced coffee would be more welcome.*

Writing in my journal that morning, I was fussing about the heat and how I did not have the proper clothing. I was interrupted by a knock on the door, and the maid asked if she might come in to clean the room. "Certainly," I said as I greeted her with a pleasant voice, as if I had not just been complaining to God.

"Are you having a good day?" I inquired.

"Not so good," she responded.

"Is there anything I can do?" I asked.

"Oh, no. Somebody just stole sixty dollars from me, and I say stole 'cause I did not give permission for them to take it."

Immediately, a small voice spoke inside my heart reminding me that I had sixty dollars in my purse. I am not used to traveling around the country giving away money, so I ignored the thought! Asking her a few more questions about herself, I hurried on to ask if she went to church in the neighborhood, thinking I could get her in touch with a minister who might help her with the money.

"No. Not since I was a child." She continued. "You see, my rent money is due. I live in a neighborhood where you have to board up the windows and double lock the doors, and women get abused and robbed all the time. But it's the only place I can afford right now."

She now had my full attention. Just minutes before she walked into my room, I was complaining about the awful heat in the safety and security of a hotel room. Once again I offered to help, but she insisted there was nothing I could do. That small voice was still whispering to my heart.

I called her by name, which was on her name tag. "Patti, you said you don't go to church anywhere in the community?"

"Oh, no. Not since I was a small child."

Bravely, I said, "Patti, has anyone ever told you about Jesus? Or would you say you are in the process of discovering who He is?"

"No one has ever told me about Him. Can He help?"

While I caught my thoughts, she kept talking. "Will you tell me about Him?"

There I was . . . Bible in hand . . . having my quiet time. I stammered out these words: "Well sure, I can tell you about Jesus, but don't you think we should ask your supervisor if we can take the time to talk?" You see, Patti was on company time. So was I.

"Oh, my supervisor won't mind. She has already been praying for me."

Wow! Her response should not have surprised me in the least. This was a divine appointment. We can trust that the Holy Spirit is already working ahead of us.

I invited her to sit beside me on the bed and I showed her Romans 3:23: "For all have sinned and fall short of the glory of God." And Romans 5:8: "But God demonstrates His own love toward us, in that while we were still sinners, Christ died for us." And Romans 6:23: "The wages of sin is death, but the free gift of God is eternal life." And finally Romans 10:9–10: "That if you confess with your mouth Jesus as Lord, and believe in your heart that God raised Him from the dead, you shall be saved; for with the heart man believes, resulting in righteousness, and with the mouth he confesses, resulting in salvation."

She quietly prayed the prayer to invite Christ into her heart. When we finished, she jumped up immediately and said, "I must clean your room!"

"Don't bother," I offered, since I had already made the bed.

"Well, I'll at least do the bathroom." When she walked to the bathroom, you guessed it, my heart knew I was going to give her the sixty dollars. I went into my suitcase and got the money and a small card and wrote her a note, asking her to read the little tract I enclosed in the envelope when she got home that evening. When she finished the bathroom, I gave her the envelope and said, "Patti, will you promise me that you will not open this note until you get home tonight?" She agreed. That felt safe to me.

When she left my room, I realized it was 8:30 in the morning— the exact time my senior adult friends, Ruth Fennell and Ida Richards, always prayed for my daily travel calendar. When they prayed, God opened the heavens and brought glory to Himself by working through us. So I picked up the phone to call my prayer partners, and as I dialed the number, another knock came to the door. Hanging up the phone, I went to the door to find Patti standing there. She said, "I came back to tell you something." I invited her inside. She said, "I feel so clean all over."

"Patti, that is just how you feel when Jesus comes to live in your life. It does feel clean all over."

"Well, there's something else too."

"What is it?" I asked, wondering what she would say.

"When you read to me from that book, that one"—she said, looking around the room and pointing to my Bible—"that one over there, I felt something coming from you to me."

What a joy it was to tell her that that was the Holy Spirit, and He was God's gift to her in giving her power. Women, God's Holy Spirit goes before us daily in our lives, empowering us to trust Him to work through our lives. Imagine my joy when Patti shared that her supervisor had already been praying for her. We can trust the Holy Spirit works in our lives just as He worked in the lives of Cornelius and Peter. The Teacher—the Guide—goes before us in everything we do.

Trust that truth! There is nowhere you can go but that the Holy Spirit is not already there. Add this truth to your heart. He, the Holy Spirit indwells you. He clothes you with Himself and clothes Himself with you. His holy presence in you draws people to Christ. He is responsible to draw them to Himself—through you.

Pentecost was for you and me as well as for the early disciples. The same Holy Spirit comes to us in our salvation . . . clothing us with Himself.

John 16:8 says, "And He, when He comes, will convict the world concerning sin, and righteousness, and judgment." Aren't you glad you are not in charge of convicting people of sin and judgment? The work of the Holy Spirit is to bring the person from death to life.

Think back to the day that you asked Jesus to come into your heart. The tender voice of the Holy Spirit drew you into His presence. The prayer you prayed to receive the gift of salvation was first placed in your heart by the Holy Spirit, calling you to Christ.

People often question how a person can come to know God if he or she has never heard the story. Romans 1:19–20 clearly states that they are without excuse:

> That which is known about God is evident within them; for God made it evident to them. For since the creation of the world, His invisible attributes, His eternal power and divine nature, have been clearly seen, being understood through what has been made, so that they are without excuse.

Since the creation of the world, the Spirit of God has been making Himself known to man.

- God uses nature to reveal Himself.
- God uses music to reveal His symphony of grace.
- God uses art and literature to show His creative hand.
- God uses life experiences to reveal His ever-present existence.
- God uses people as instruments of His power to exhibit the fruits of the Spirit revealing the truth of the Spirit.

Part of the work of the Holy Spirit is to reveal the truth of God's very existence.

THE ACTS OF THE HOLY SPIRIT

I can't wait for you to see the acts of the Holy Spirit in the book of Acts. It has mystery, in the appearing of the Spirit. It has miracles, through ordinary disciples, full of Spirit power. It has extravagant love, displayed in church sharing. It has extraordinary worship, in powerful praying. It has eternal implications, for the Gentile nation. It has jail scenes and angel gatekeepers. It has my attention! Nothing can block the power of the Holy Spirit in the Acts of the Holy Spirit. Nothing at Pentecost! Nothing now!

I heard a pastor give a great outline for the book of Acts. He said in chapter 1, the Savior went up. In chapter 2, the Spirit came down. In chapter 3 and following, the saints went out. It is simple and profound. Someone said the book of Acts should be named the Acts of the Holy Spirit.

In Acts 1:4–8, after the resurrection, Jesus commands His disciples not to leave Jerusalem but to wait for what the Father had promised. They questioned Him about the time He would restore the kingdom of Israel. The Greek meanings for the word *wait* are "time," "opportune time," and "God's destined time."

Jesus responded, "It is not for you to know times or epochs [God's destined time] which the Father has fixed by His own authority; but you shall receive power when the Holy Spirit has come upon you; and you shall be My witnesses both in Jerusalem, and in all Judea and Samaria, and even to the remotest part of the earth" (vv. 7–8). Perhaps He meant all time, opportune time, and destined time for His work. He asked them to wait until they were clothed with the Holy Spirit.

As they waited, they heard something.

Acts 2:2: "And suddenly there came from heaven a noise like a violent, rushing wind, and it filled the whole house where they were sitting." They heard the rushing wind. Remember that John said we don't know where it (the wind of the Spirit) comes from— or where it is going. But they heard it that day! This is one of the ways the Spirit works.

As they waited, they saw something.

Acts 2:3: "And there appeared to them tongues as of fire distributing [being distributed] themselves, and they rested on each one of them." The Scripture says they saw what appeared to be as fire—which sat down on each one of their heads. What a sight that must have been—each one clothed in the fire of the Holy Spirit. No wonder the early church turned the world upside down.

As they waited, they felt something.

Verse 4 says, "And they were all filled with the Holy Spirit." They felt the all-consuming power of the Holy Spirit filling them that day, and they each began to speak in their own language. This event was so powerful, the Jews living in Jerusalem, gathered when this sound occurred, and they marveled and were amazed. The followers were full of the Holy Spirit. In fact, these Christians were so full of the Holy Spirit's power, some in the observing community thought they were drunk, or full of sweet wine, as the Scripture says. They were acting under the controlling power of the Holy Spirit.

After they waited, they said something.

Pentecost changed Peter the most. He took the stand, raised his voice, and preached a strong message right from the prophet Joel. When he finished, the people in the crowd were so touched, they asked what they needed to do to get this power. Peter said, "Repent . . . be baptized . . . receive the gift of the Holy Spirit" (v. 38). Three thousand responded that day. Peter preached under the authority and power of the Holy Spirit.

After they waited, they did something.

The church responded as the church always will respond to the working of the Holy Spirit. Verses 42–43: "And they were continually devoting themselves to the apostles' teaching and to fellowship, to the breaking of bread and to prayer. And everyone kept feeling a sense of awe; and many wonders and signs were taking place through the apostles."

As the church met, they prayed, and when they had prayed, the place where they prayed was shaken. How long has it been since your place of prayer was shaken? They prayed and then they spoke boldly the word of God. This situation describes Paul's words: "To know the love of Christ which surpasses knowledge, that you may be filled up to all the fullness of God" (Eph. 3:19). Oh, my sisters in Christ, that is what I desire and know you desire in your life—to be filled to all the fullness of Christ, empowered to live daily in His presence in all our circumstances.

THE AUTHORITY OF THE HOLY SPIRIT

A desire of my heart would have been to meet Corrie ten Boom in person. Corrie was a woman who lived in the authority of the Holy Spirit. The closest I would ever get to her was to have the privilege of visiting her childhood home in Holland, reading her books, and seeing the movie *The Hiding Place*.

After taking a tour in her home several years ago, my friend and I decided to take tea in the little shop across the street from the ten Boom home. As we sat down, my friend Jo laughingly accused me of standing so close to the sofa in the family room that she guessed I was tempted to sit down on it. She was right. As we walked the cobblestone streets to the church, I thought to myself, *Maybe she stepped here and here and here.* It was a time of remembering what God's Spirit had done in one life that was totally committed to Him.

The story says that the lives of over eight hundred Jewish people were saved because of Corrie ten Boom and her family. I whispered in my own heart, *God, use me as you used Miss Corrie.* I heard a friend of Corrie's tell about the time she visited Manly Beesley in the hospital on one of the occasions before his death. Manley said, "Talking to Corrie was being privy to her conversation with God. She would be talking to you—then look up and talk with God a while—then turn back and pick back up the conversation with you." She was so intimately acquainted with her heavenly Father, she carried on a running conversation with Him hourly.

During this particular hospital visit the phone rang. It was the

Billy Graham Organization tracking her down to tell her they would have to stop the movie production of *The Hiding Place* due to lack of funds. Miss Corrie's response was this: "That is no problem. It is God's will for the movie to be made. We are being obedient, so continue with the film."

The voice on the phone said, "We can't. We are out of money."

"That's no problem. My Father owns the cattle on a thousand hills," she said and hung up. It wasn't long until a Texas rancher sold some cattle and sent the money to the Graham Organization—designated for this film. Corrie lived so in tune with the authority and power of the Holy Spirit.

The Great Commission, as many call Matthew 28:18–20, calls us to trust His authority given to us from His command:

> And Jesus came up and spoke to them, saying, "All authority has been given to Me in heaven and on earth. Go therefore and make disciples of all the nations, baptizing them in the name of the Father and the Son and the Holy Spirit, teaching them to observe all that I commanded you; and lo, I am with you always, even to the end of the age."

The promise of the power comes in the presence of the Spirit, "Lo, I am with you always." Trusting the Holy Spirit comes when we understand the Holy Spirit is the authority and He gives us boldness and wisdom.

After Peter's great message, the disciples healed a man. The response of the crowd was this: "Now as they observed the confidence of Peter and John, and understood that they were uneducated and untrained men, they were marveling, and began to recognize them as having been with Jesus" (Acts 4:13). What a profound testimony. I believe when a woman's life is clothed with the authority of the Holy Spirit, her circle of influence will recognize that she has been with Jesus. You perhaps have been in the presence of such a woman. You feel drawn into her spirit and refreshed by His Spirit, and when that happens God gets the glory.

Acts 4:7–8 tells us, "And when they had placed them in the center, they began to inquire, 'By what power, or in what name, have you done this?' Then Peter, filled with the Holy Spirit," preached a bold message.

You and I must learn to trust the authority and power of the Holy Spirit in our lives. In Luke 12:11–12, the Holy Spirit is referred to as the teacher: "And when they bring you before the synagogues and the rulers and the authorities, do not become anxious about how or what you should speak in your defense, or what you should say; for the Holy Spirit will teach you in that very hour what you ought to say."

James 1:5 gives us more encouragement: "But if any of you lacks wisdom, let him ask of God, who gives to all men generously and without reproach, and it will be given to him."

I was flying home from a meeting in Idaho, and just as I got seated on the plane, a young woman who was expecting a child came and sat in the seat beside me. The young woman, whose name was Kim, asked me if I was afraid to fly. I told her I was no longer afraid to fly, having flown almost two million miles on Delta Air Lines! She told me how frightened she was—and that she was on her way to a family funeral. She had never flown before.

I gave her a little pep talk about planes and added that I had prayed that morning, using Psalm 91:11 (my travel verse): "He will give His angels charge concerning you, to guard you." Kim said that she had also prayed that morning, so I asked about her faith background. She shared that she was a Christian but that her husband was not and she was praying for him. Just before the plane departed, the flight attendant, who was aware of my companion's fear of flying, checked on her one more time. I assured her that I would help Kim as the plane took off and that I had prayed for God's protection early that morning.

Sara, the flight attendant said, "I do that every morning I fly." She then promised she would get right back to Kim after the plane got into the air.

Kim's fear was so strong she would not even lean over to look out the window. I thought she might squeeze my hand off as the plane taxied down the runway and lifted into the air. As we leveled off, Sara came back to offer Kim something to drink. She thanked me for being willing to help, and I responded that it was my pleasure. "I believe I was to sit by Kim today to show God's care to her as she has a very difficult day ahead getting to the funeral."

Sara said, "I knew you were a Christian. I saw you on this flight yesterday. You had your Bible and a notebook open. I told my cabin mates that you were a Christian speaker. And besides, you had on that same purple dress!" We laughed about the dress as I assured her that I was indeed a Christian speaker and that Kim told me she was praying for her husband to know Christ.

I thought Sara would jump out of her uniform. She promised again to come back after she served the beverages. When she came back she told me where she lived, and we discovered her pastor was a good friend of mine. Sara turned to Kim and shared how her Bible study group offered her friendship and began to pray for her husband, which eventually led him to Christ. She was so full of excitement as she told Kim her husband's story, and every person in the first two rows heard about Christ—boldly—from this Christian flight attendant.

Women can trust that the Spirit of God will give them the words to say and the wisdom and tenderness with which to say them.

THE FILLING OF THE HOLY SPIRIT

Think back to a recent Bible lesson or retreat in which you were the leader or teacher. You spent much time in preparation and prayer. When the event or lesson was over, how did you feel?

Depleted? You probably physically dropped your shoulders and gave out a deep sigh. Why? You had relied on the power of the Holy Spirit to lead and teach. Or, you might say, you used the Spirit's power. That's why D. L. Moody said, "We leak"! So as you walk from Bible study to church or pack the car after the retreat, you bow again before the Father and breathe in, asking the Holy Spirit to fill you once again. The power of the Holy Spirit does not leave us since He indwells us, but we must continually ask for Him to refill us, if you please, just as when a car runs out of gas it needs to be refilled. There is nothing wrong with the car, except that it has used up the supply of fuel and needs refueling!

We are probably not as comfortable accepting the filling of the Holy Spirit as we are trusting that He empowers, teaches, corrects, and guides us. The filling of the Holy Spirit is a day-by-day, moment-by-moment process. The God of the Old Testament refers often to Israel as a people for His own possession. The filling of the Holy Spirit is to be possessed by the Holy Spirit.

Ephesians 5:18 reads, "And do not get drunk with wine, for that is dissipation, but be filled with the Spirit." This means when you pray, "be being filled" with the Spirit. It is a continual process. If we are under the influence of wine, the wine is controlling our behavior. But the drink will wear off after a while. Paul suggests that we be continually filled . . . a process of becoming a God-possessed people.

To be filled with the Holy Spirit means to be surrendered to Him—allowing Him to think His thoughts in us and releasing His power through us. C. S. Lewis, in his book *Mere Christianity*, said the "Holy Spirit empowering us is the difference between paint which is merely laid on the surface, and a dye or stain, which soaks right through."

So often before or after Jesus would heal or bless someone, the Scriptures record that He went alone to pray, got up early to pray, or prayed all night. Jesus knew the source of power. Keep in mind that you continue in Christ, that is, you live by faith just as you received Him as Lord. Your Spirit-filled life is given and maintained by God.

How Can You Be Filled with the Holy Spirit?

Satisfy is defined as, "to fulfill the needs and desire of." As you and I seek after, spend time on, and pursue a right relationship with the heavenly Father, our needs and desires will be satisfied.

It is easy for most of us to understand who the Spirit is and how the Spirit works, but we have many questions about how to be filled with the Spirit. It's amazing because we recognize persons whose lives are touched by the Holy Spirit, yet we don't see ourselves in that place by simply having the desire to be intimate with Christ. Jesus says in Matthew 5:6, "Blessed [healthy] are those who hunger and thirst for righteousness, for they shall be satisfied." Ask God to put the desire in you to live in the fullness of Christ.

Perhaps the most significant act on our part in this process is the continual journey of confessions. A vessel open to confessing, cleansing, and being forgiven, over and over, is empty and ready for filling.

First John 1:9 teaches: "If we confess our sins, He is faithful and righteous to forgive us our sins and to cleanse us from all unrighteousness." I've heard preachers say that when they were students in seminary, Bertha Smith, when on campus, would walk up to them, point her finger in their faces, and say, "Are you prayed up? Are your sins confessed?" The students were annoyed at her courage, but many ended up on their knees in confession before God.

Bertha Smith says, in her writing about the Holy Spirit, "to be filled with the Spirit, you must acknowledge some absolute essentials."

- You must give testimony. Share spiritual blessings. Cease to tell and soon there will be nothing to tell. I believe we lack a clear witness when we do not live and talk about the joy we know in Christ.

- You must constantly remind yourself that by nature you are no better than when you were saved. We have this treasure in earthen vessels. Why? That our new, miraculous lives will be of God, and we will get no glory for them. We must form new habits in light of our new position in Christ: systematic Bible study and prayer, and habits of keeping all sin confessed up-to-date. Confess immediately (this is necessary for the sake of future testimony).

- You must keep going on with the Lord daily. A Spirit-filled life is a must to keep walking in Christ. Howard Ramsey, a precious friend and mentor, says you can never tell another about Christ when there is sin in your own life. It just chokes you. In other words, the Holy Spirit can't flow through you because of this sin. Therefore, confession is necessary and critical to the filling. As in a good marriage: when you are upset about something your mate did and are holding your mate at a distance, the love can't flow through your anger or hurt. Until you ask or give forgiveness, the love between you is choked and can't get out.

When there is sin present in life, it is almost as if we hide from intimacy with God. When we get in God's presence, the Holy Spirit reveals truth to us through the Scripture, a devotional guide, or a friend, and the convicting presence of the Holy Spirit draws us to confess and be cleansed. As in marriage or friendship, when finally one of the two asks for forgiveness, the cleansing power flows freely and draws them back into intimacy. The confession for me is daily, hourly, moment by moment.

I had been on the road several days, and my husband, Bob, came to meet me at the airport. This was a real treat for me, so after we had gotten my luggage, we went out to eat. I was so aware that I needed to get home and wash a load of clothes in order to pack for the next day's journey, that I became anxious. The check came and we just kept sitting there until finally I said, "Let's pay and leave."

He said, "You're paying, aren't you?"

"No, I'm not."

"Yes, you said you would treat me this time."

"No, I didn't."

"Well, I didn't even bring in my wallet."

"That's some excuse!"

He got up, went to the car to get his wallet, and paid the bill . . . and we drove home in total silence. Any conversation between us was over. The joy was gone. The delight wasn't there. I was sure he was wrong, and he was just as sure I was wrong—all over a few dollars.

When I got home, I began unpacking and repacking my suitcase. Did you know you can make a lot of noise packing—if you want someone to notice? He ignored me. Climbing into bed later that night, I lay there replaying what had happened. This was not how I'd envisioned our time together. I remembered . . . that small whisper again . . . that indeed I had promised I would pay!

Then I could see myself the next day standing up in front of women talking to them about splashing the living water. Slowly I moved closer to his side and said I was wrong and asked forgiveness. Oh, yes! Forgiveness . . . cleansed from unrighteous behavior. You're thinking, *that's a small thing.* Have you ever noticed the small things catch us off guard and keep us from being the presence of Christ to each other? At our house, confession is almost daily!

The filling of the Holy Spirit comes when we desire to be filled, confess our sin, and submit our will to God's will. Our culture is not comfortable with the word *submit.* Someone has suggested that *submit* means to "honor another by putting their needs and desires before my own to please Christ." Living a Spirit-filled life is to honor Christ by dying to self and putting His desires before my own. Paul, in Romans 12:1, calls us to do that: "I urge you therefore, brethren [sisters], by the mercies of God, to present your bodies a living and holy sacrifice, acceptable [well pleasing] to God, which is your spiritual service of worship."

What a powerful statement . . . called to give my life as a sacrifice in an act of worship to God, submitting to His authority in my life.

Oswald Chambers said it very clearly: "The one and only characteristic of the Holy Ghost in a man is a strong family-likeness to Jesus Christ, and freedom from everything that is unlike Him. Are we prepared to set ourselves apart for the Holy Spirit's ministrations in us?"

As John the Baptist introduced Jesus to the crowds, he said of his relationship to Jesus: "He must increase, but I must decrease" (John 3:30). John knew he belonged to Jesus, and he did not confuse his leadership role. His role was to prepare the people for Jesus. Gordon MacDonald says of John, in his book *Ordering Your Private World*, "If there was a moment when the crowd's praise became thunderous, the voice of God from within was even louder." MacDonald says that voice spoke more convincingly because John had first ordered his inner world out in the desert. Listening to that inner voice of the Spirit orders our private world and gives focus to our call as Christians. Proverbs 4:23: "Watch over your heart with all diligence, for from it flow the springs of life."

Our submission comes from that quiet place where our lives are ordered in His will. Out of the quiet order, we receive the filling, the clothing by the Holy Spirit. Submission—like confession—is daily, moment by moment, dying to self. No wonder the little boy asked Miss 'Quater if she was God; he saw a life clothed with the Holy Spirit.

Several years ago at a conference center in New Mexico, I was teaching about the work of the Holy Spirit. The women became very excited about the idea of being clothed in the Spirit. As the week came to an end, I made my way back to the hotel. When I stepped into my room, I found a note under the door. That note became a blessing in my life. I was very touched and humbled that God chose to use me in this woman's life. I looked for her address on the envelope so I could write and thank her for her encouragement. I found no address, but on the flap of the envelope were these words, *I know you're not God, but you sure are wearing His clothes.* My heart cried out, *No! No! Not me!* Oh, my . . . Yes! Yes! Every child of God is clothed in the presence and power of the Holy Spirit!

SPLASHING IN THE FREEDOM OF THE SPIRIT

1. Can you recognize the work of the Holy Spirit in your life? Give examples.

2. How have you seen God work in the life of a person who does not know Christ?

3. Describe a person you know who is clothed in the power of the Holy Spirit.

4. List some Holy Spirit characteristics in her life.

5. Read 1 Corinthians 12. List the varieties of gifts of the Spirit.

6. Describe your gift. How can you use it in the body of Christ?

MORE SPLASHING: Read R. C. Sproul's *The Mystery of the Holy Spirit* (Carol Stream, IL: Tyndale House, 1994) and Gordon MacDonald's *Renewing Your Spiritual Passion* (Nashville: Oliver-Nelson, 1986).

6

THE WELLSPRING
OF FAMILY WORSHIP

We always sat in the first pew—piano side—in my growing-up church. At that time I am sure my sister and I and two brothers were seated there so *both* our parents could watch us carefully and discipline us if necessary! With four small children, no nursery, and minister-father on the platform, Mother always sat in the middle of the four children. At that time, she had one three-year-old, twin two-year-olds, and one one-year-old . . . and that's the truth! Only PKs (preacher kids) could understand *the look* in the eyes of their preacher-daddy as he sat on the pulpit platform. It was nearly always a spanking look. I remember it like it was yesterday.

Following big church, we walked home. Well, to be honest, we walked everywhere in those days. The parsonage, which was the house provided for the minister and his family, was on the same property as the church, and only about fifty steps away.

I recall as an older child that the walk home was quiet, and you can be sure the child expecting the rod was the quietest. The wooden sidewalk from the house to behind the shed was well worn. Before he administered the belt, my father would tell us that it would hurt him more than it did us. That speech did not make sense to me—until I had children of my own. Even more today, I know how it must grieve our heavenly Father when, as His children, we disobey His laws.

Some fourteen years later, a sister was born into our Milligan family, making five children! I claim the privilege of being the middle child since my twin brother is six and one-half hours older than I am. I was the peacemaker in our family. I am sure that if my siblings were writing this book, they would add that I was also the tattletale. But, you understand, if I was in charge of the peace, I always had to be on the lookout for the troublemakers.

I recall a day *all* of us were getting spanked, and I cried out, "But I didn't do anything!"

My father replied, "Then this is just in case you do."

When I remind my parents about this event, they always say to look how well we all turned out! So there you have it for raising children in the early days.

There were rules in my home. Here are just a few of them:

- Remember that children are to be seen and not heard.
- Watch your manners.
- Do your chores.
- Respect your elders.
- Never say "shut up."
- Remember the Sabbath day to keep it holy.
- Always tell the truth.
- Do your best and then some.
- Finish what you begin.
- Take piano lessons, sing, or learn to play an instrument.

- Study hard for good grades.

- Always remember that you are a Milligan!

I always felt that the last rule came straight from the mouth of my grandmother; we should live in such a way as to bring honor to the family name. That may be old-fashioned, but I choose to feel that a high standard was set for us by our parents and grandparents, who taught us that the heavenly Father also called us to show a family resemblance by honoring and obeying Him.

My parents' rule about celebrating the Sabbath, or Sunday, had the most impact on us. The Sabbath was a holy day in my growing-up home. My mother always cooked Sunday dinner on Saturday evening. We cleaned the house on Saturday so it would be presentable on Sabbath. Everyone had specific jobs. The reason I remember this was because I was sure my sister always got the easier job. Even as Mother, in disgust, changed our responsibilities from time to time and switched our chores, I was still certain Moyra got the easier part. I can still taste the dust on that long, hardwood rail staircase, which had to be done with a hand cloth, and knowing the mother inspector would follow up to see if I had done well. If I hadn't, I would have to do it over again to please her. After all, company just might drop by.

It was a really big event when we got to wear our church clothes, and everything had to be readied on Saturday night. Clothes were pressed and hung . . . shoes were shined . . . socks were folded . . . Bible and offering were laid out—all in preparation for Sabbath morning. Sunday school lessons were prepared on Saturday . . . and getting all four children to study their lessons was a task. It was a ritual upon which we counted. I'm sure it must have made Sunday morning a bit easier for our mom, getting our large family ready to go to church—on time.

On Saturday night, the dining room table was set in preparation for Sunday dinner with the good dishes—not fine china, mind you, because we didn't have any! We did have good dishes. We put on a nice tablecloth and the good glassware. As you can tell, we dressed up for Sunday—our home as well as ourselves. We tried to present the best to the Father. It was not about showing off—it was just the way our family celebrated Sabbath.

As you might now guess, we were not allowed to play on Sabbath day! We were allowed Sunday toys—quiet games like puzzles. We could also read good books like the Sugar Creek Gang or the Hardy Boys, or we could read the Bible. As teens, this was difficult because our friends were allowed to play ball or go to the park. For the Milligan children, it was a day for quiet rest in our home.

Each morning during the week, we were called to breakfast, and we gathered around the breakfast table. While the porridge got cold, my father opened his Bible and read the Word of God to us. As a child I often wondered if he read all of the Old Testament.

After Father read, we would then move from the table, get down on our knees by our chairs, and Father would pray for each one of us children by name. Then he would pray for all the missionaries by name. When the final *amen* was said, and not before, we were then free to eat breakfast. This was known as *family altar*. We did this every morning of our lives—even on Christmas morning! I remember my parents praying for very specific things in our lives—often reminding God about our personal attitudes and behavior. I once heard Chuck Swindoll say these dynamic words: "Pray over your children, and touch them even as they go out the door to school. You will be giving them a blessing for the day."

In biblical times, parents blessed their children with a physical touch . . . a spoken touch . . . and words of affirmation. In Jewish tradition, the father assumed primary responsibility for training the child. The Jewish law states: "It is the duty of every father to train his children in the practice of all the precepts."[1] My parents parented us—based their love and care for us—from Proverbs 22:6: "Train up a child in the way he should go, even when he is old he will not depart from it." To a strict Jew, that meant the way of his father and his father's father. Every Jewish child learned Deuteronomy 4:6–9. Parents taught their children God's law as instructed in Deuteronomy 6:1–7.

Donald Whitney, in his *Spiritual Disciplines for the Christian Life*, says: "One of the main reasons for a lack of Godliness is prayerlessness." I would say that prayer was the cornerstone in our home in my growing-up years. My brothers, sisters, and I have a great family heritage in prayer. Every day as long as I can remember, my parents would pray for each of their children by name. They later added all the grandchildren and then the great-grandchildren. My father has a bit of an English accent, and when he prays, I would feel as if I was in the very presence of God. I often say we were raised at our mother's knees—and over our dad's knees. My mother related everything to the Scripture. She was not a highly educated woman, but she was a well-read woman, and she loved the Word of God.

My mother was a woman of prayer. One day in a visit with her before she passed away, she asked me this question: "Esther, do you ever speak to ministers' wives?"

"Yes, sometimes," was my reply.

"Well, I shared with a group of young women recently that every Sabbath morning, I would lay out your father's clothes on the bed for him—his suit, tie, hankie, socks, and shoes." She said that she was surprised when they laughed at her because she had not intended to be humorous. Their response was, *Let the men dress themselves!*

"I remember you did that for Dad. Why did you do it?" I thought it might be a rule in some minister's wife's handbook!

She replied quietly with these piercing words: "I did it so that your father could have more time in prayer before God as he prepared to go to the pulpit and open the Word of God for the people of God."

I came away from that conversation feeling deeply convicted. I did not serve my husband in that manner. So—you guessed it—the very next Sunday, I got up a bit earlier. While Bob was having a bite of breakfast with the children, I went into our bedroom and laid out a suit, shirt, tie, hankie, socks, and shoes on the bed for him. I felt so proud. He came to the bedroom to get dressed, saw the suit, shirt, tie, etcetera and said, "What on earth are you doing?"

"I'm laying out your clothes for you."

"Thanks, but I've been dressing myself on Sundays for all these years in our marriage, and I really don't need any assistance."

"I was just trying to help and, besides, I think you are supposed to be praying!"

We laughed as I shared what my mother had told me about putting out my father's clothes. I believe this servant gift of my mother's was an act of worship to God. I have since pondered what might happen in the homes of the pastors all across the world if wives did something on Sabbath morning to make it possible for their minister/husbands to have more time on their knees before God as they prepared to speak the Word of God to the people of God.

Being a woman of this new century, I have also wondered how the family might be affected if on Monday morning the father would get the lunches ready and help with breakfast—so the mother could be on her knees in prayer for her children as they go off to school that day and for her husband as he goes to the work-place. I believe we would see a difference in our children . . . our husbands . . . and the school systems!

One of the great truths in John 4 is the awesome news Jesus reveals about true worship, as He and the Samaritan woman have a dialogue about worship. She learned a profound truth the day she met Jesus at the well. She, like many of us, thought of worship as a place, and not as a person. In my family of origin, *our* place of worship was *church*. My childlike mind associated God with church. In fact my early memory of God is related to the Baptist church in

Crossfield, a small town close to Calgary, Alberta, Canada—the church were I met Jesus Christ as my personal Savior.

A child learns early that church is one of the places where he goes to worship God. Parents need to help the child recognize, at the right time, that worship is not a place; rather, it is a personal relationship. I saw a church ad in the paper that said: "The ultimate sanctuary is not a place . . . but a Person."

The Samaritan woman made the person connection at the well that day. She and Jesus were having what I would call a religious conversation about Jacob's well and the coming Messiah. Read His words in John 4:21–24:

> Woman, believe me, an hour is coming when neither in this mountain, nor in Jerusalem, shall you worship the Father. You worship that which you do not know; we worship that which we know, for salvation is from the Jews. But an hour is coming, and now is, when the true worshipers shall worship the Father in spirit and truth; for such people the Father seeks to be His worshipers. God is spirit, and those who worship Him must worship in spirit and truth.

What profound words to a woman who was not allowed to worship in the inner temple; being a Samaritan woman she was shunned by the Messiah's own people. Those were indeed profound words! Look what happened next. The woman had enough religious background information to say, "I know that Messiah is coming . . . when that One comes, He will declare all things to us" (v. 25). Jesus, the Messiah, said to her, "I who speak to you am He."

A literal translation would read: "The One who speaks to you is I AM." She and the Messiah—together in worship! Jesus chose to reveal Himself to a woman . . . a Samaritan woman. Amazing Grace!

The Samaritan woman was challenged by Jesus to consider

who He was. Because of this encounter, she was to become the first missionary. The moment she recognized the truth of who He was, she ran to share the good news. She had met the Messiah. What an altar of worship that experience was for her!

Just as the Samaritan woman met Jesus by the well, you and I can choose to meet Jesus through family altar in our homes, expecting our children to encounter Him personally in their lives.

THE PURPOSE OF FAMILY ALTAR

My husband and I chose to celebrate the tradition of family altar differently from both of our families of origin. We chose to celebrate family altar once a week, except for the holiday months of Christmas and Thanksgiving. Most often we made it part of our family night activity. We worked together as teams—the guys, the gals, and the parents—to make plans for worship. Often that was as meaningful as the altar time. We'd gather at the kitchen table or in the family room to share in a time of worship. We used music, Scripture, dialogue, and story time as our elements of worship. All family members took turns praying. Our children laugh now and say, they could always tell when it was a special time 'cause Mom cried.

We firmly believe God's instruction in Deuteronomy 6:4–9:

Hear, O Israel! The Lord is our God, the Lord is one! And you shall love the Lord your God with all your heart and with all your soul and with all your might. And these words, which I am commanding you today, shall be on your heart; and you shall teach them diligently to your sons [and daughters] and shall talk of them when you sit in your house and when you walk by the way and when you lie down and when you rise up. And you shall bind them as a sign on your hand and they shall be as frontals on your forehead. And you shall write them on the doorposts of your house and on your gates.

It is the responsibility of the parents to give religious instruction to the children. The church can and will assist ... but the primary work is for the parents! This is very difficult in today's culture where in many families both parents work outside and inside the home. Richard Foster, the wonderfully thoughtful and gifted Quaker writer, said these dramatic words: "The closest thing to a family altar in America is the TV! We worship it."

USA Today reported some time ago that children watch more than thirty-seven hours of television a week, and parents talk to children about thirty-seven seconds a day, and to each other, about seven minutes a day. How can we possibly teach our children God's laws and God's ways in that kind of time frame? We can't!

Family altar builds traditions that bring solidarity in the home. The earlier the family can begin the tradition of family altar, the easier it will be to maintain it, even during the teen years. The experts tell us today that the father can have an impact on his children while they are still in the mother's womb by talking to them and playing music for them.

Many years ago, I was visiting in the home of a young couple who were in the army and stationed in Germany. Their little baby was just six weeks old. Every evening when the child was put to bed, the young father stood at his crib and read the Bible to him. You might wonder what impact could that possibly have. First, from birth, the father took time with the baby and the baby loved his daddy's voice. Second, the Word of God is the *Word of God.* What better reading could there be? And that child is now in college—living a Christ-centered life.

Establishing family altar as a tradition in your home takes a huge commitment to obey God's commands. Most often, the work load for this commitment will fall to the mother. In biblical times, Jewish boys were taught by their father, and by the age of thirteen, started wearing phylacteries, *tefillin,* during weekday morning prayers. Phylacteries were two black leather cubes with long leather straps. The cubes encased passages from the Torah written on strips of parchment. At the beginning of the day, those prayers were said. You might think that a strange tradition, but that very tradition taught young men the Scripture.

We already know that children learn from repetition. If we therefore teach them God's Word at family altar, fulfilling our purpose (binding God's word in our hearts), we are building into their hearts and eventually into their lives the truth of Deuteronomy 6:4–9.

Because family altar was a tradition in our home, we observed it whether everyone wanted to observe it or not. Our children did not have a choice in this matter. Family altar is one of those items parents control by virtue of being the parent, and it wields power just in the fact that a tradition does not have to be explained—just done.

We used the calendar year to help make preparation for worship. For example, we have always had a worship service following our Thanksgiving meal. It has always been a very special time to which we looked forward because of the creativity and planning that always goes into this service. Everyone who joined our family circle around that Thanksgiving table was involved in this service with us because we always have a response time. As our children grew older, they were given responsibility for helping to plan and produce the worship time—with the help of their dad.

As children come into the teen years, they may not be happy about family altar times. Such was the case in our home. Yes, it feels uncomfortable, and maybe even forced, but based on our belief and on many, many good experiences, we forged right ahead. I will never forget one such occasion that proved rewarding.

When our daughter, Melody, came home for Thanksgiving from her first semester at the University of Alabama, my parents, my baby sister, and her husband were celebrating with us. I will never forget the day! I had asked Bob to go a bit easy on the thankful response time . . . knowing the circumstances of family members present on this special day. He was very sensitive in his statement. His statement went something like this:

"I know everyone here has much for which to be thankful this year, so why don't I just voice a prayer of thanks for all of us."

We were all startled at what happened next!

"Wait, just a minute!" said Melody! "I have something to say. I wish no one was here except Mom, Dad, and Big Dave, 'cause what I want to say is none of anyone's darn (that's not really what she said) business but mine."

Eyes open wide, I took a big breath and glanced over at my mother, wondering what on earth she was thinking about this outburst in our worship time. My heart was quickly quieted with my daughter's next words.

"This time last year, and probably the year before, I hated this family altar stuff. But now that I'm in college and I've experienced a lot of things and been with kids whose homes are not at all like mine, I want to say thank you for always having family altar—'cause it's made our home different and I have come to appreciate it. [Long pause.] I'm done, Dad. Now you can pray."

That was prayer enough for me. Traditions don't have to be explained. It's tradition . . . and you do it . . . building solidarity in the home . . . centered at the altar of worship. Parents, be faithful to your altar time in your homes.

THE FOCUS OF FAMILY ALTAR

"By this you shall know that the living God is among you" (Josh 3:10). "And the priests who carried the ark of the covenant of the LORD stood firm on dry ground in the middle of the Jordan while all Israel crossed on dry ground, until all the nation had finished crossing the Jordan" (v. 17). Then God instructed Joshua to take twelve men—one from each tribe—and tell each to take twelve stones and place the stones by their tents. He said: "Let this be a sign among you, so that when your children ask later, saying, 'What do these stones mean to you?' then you shall say to them, 'Because the waters of the Jordan were cut off before the ark of the covenant of the LORD . . . These stones shall become a memorial to the sons of Israel forever'" (4:6–7).

Earlier, when the sons of Israel were camped by the Jordan, the officers went through the camp telling the people that when they saw the ark of the covenant going through their camp, they could follow it. Then Joshua said to Israel: "Consecrate yourselves, for tomorrow the LORD will do wonders among you" (3:5).

God spoke to Joshua, telling him: "I will begin to exalt you in the sight of all Israel, that they may know that just as I have been with Moses, I will be with you" (3:7). Imagine Joshua's joy when he said in verses 9–10: "Come here, and hear the words of the LORD your God . . . 'By this you shall know that the living God is among you'!

What a great word for families today. Family altar helps families experience God working in the home. Then we, too, can say the living God is among us!

Recently, my daughter's family made a move to another city. I suggested to her that they include their three girls in their prayers about the selling of the Atlanta home and the buying of a new home . . . and in finding the right church . . . and the right school. My thinking was that as they prayed together, the girls would come to see God at work in every situation.

I began to pray Psalm 37:3–7 for the children the way I learned from *The Grandmother Book,* a wonderful book now out of print, written by grandmothers Jan Stoop and Betty Southland. In this book, Betty, one of the writers said:

> I take my problem, whatever it is, and I figuratively lay it out on my hands, palms facing upward. I specifically state what it is, and then I turn my hands down, palms open, and let the problem

drop into God's hands. When I commit the problem to Him, I have relinquished my problem to the Lord.

All of us probably have trouble with that. The psalmist says to commit our ways [troubles] to the Lord and then He immediately tells us to trust Him to take care of them. Betty goes on to say:

It is immediately at this point that I find Satan whispering his little lies in my ear, such as, "That's too minor to bother the Lord with. Why don't you just handle this one yourself?" or, "Who do you think you are that you can ask God to do that for you? So you really think He cares about that?" or "What if the Lord doesn't work it out the way you want?" The doubts and fears crop up immediately.

What does Betty do?

By an act of faith, not feelings, I simply reply, "Thank you, Lord, for I know You are taking care of my problem. Lord, I believe. Help my unbelief."

The next step is delighting in the Lord, praising Him, and thanking Him for what He can and will do. To help remember the steps of this prayer of thanks, those two grandmothers say you can use this acrostic made with the letters of the word *delight:*

Daily
Everything
Laid
Into
God's
Hands
Totally

The authors tell us to repeat this prayer over and over to remind ourselves that we have committed it to the Lord. Then we are able to move on and rest in the Lord. The psalmists say to commit, trust, delight, and finally to rest in the Lord.

Recently in my life, I have literally held my hands up to Him in adoration. I have been praying this prayer over my adult children for several months now, as well as for my grandchildren—and the line that I cry out to God so often is this: "I believe. Help my unbelief." Then I have emptied my heart into His hands with specific requests.

My prayer journal shows His faithfulness as I have marked off the requests with words of gratitude. I delighted in sharing with my daughter's family when a contract on their home was signed in just two days. I joined her family in praying as I specifically laid in God's hands the price, the place, a church, and a peace for her about the right home—that as she walked into this house, she would know it was the right home for them, and I rejoiced as they bought a home in one day . . . at the right price . . . near a good school. How wonderful to see the God of Israel at work in this place [home]. I don't know how her family celebrated this event, but "Nana" and "Bop" (our grandmother and grandfather names) made an altar of tears before the Father, thanking God that "The living God is among us" and that He is still at work so specifically in our lives.

The Tim Trinkle family's "Gramma's Summer Camp" event is inspirational. I was so impressed as mothers and children gathered each summer for one week at the grandparents' home. I was so touched by aunts teaching nieces and nephews and by cousins bonding into lifetime friends that I just knew we had to make it happen for the Burroughs clan.

In the summer of 1998 we held the first ever "Nana's Summer Camp." Our three grandgirls Anna, Caroline, and Frances—at that time ages nine, seven, and five, and their parents—came to our home in Jacksonville for four and one-half days. The "Nana's Summer Camp" signs posted on the garage door welcomed all campers with these words: *I am a promise. I am a possibility!* These words are based on God's promise to His people in Genesis 9:13: "I have set my rainbow in the clouds" (NIV). Upon entering the front door, and after hugs and kisses, they were taken to the kitchen where room assignments and all *camp rules* were posted on the kitchen cabinet doors. Camp had begun!

We learned the theme song: "I am a promise. I am a possibility. I can be anything . . . anything God wants me to be."

We read the story of Noah and the ark in preparation for a closing drama presentation we would prepare during the camp—using Noah's ark and Beanie Babies. Each morning and afternoon found us doing activities, such as designing our own camp T-shirts, going to a water park, visiting a pottery works and making our own pottery items, preparing a drama production, swimming, memorizing Scripture, fishing, and watching movies during rest time.

My favorite time was the Birthday Breakfast for all three girls. Since Bob and I are seldom with them on their real birthdays, we decided to do it all at one time. Anna helped Bop fix his famous family breakfast. Caroline set the table. Frances put the silverware on the table. After the meal and before we gave their gifts, each person was given a sheet of paper on which was drawn a gift box, wrapped in a bow with a tag that read "You are special." Anna had written the name of each person on the left-hand side of the gift box. I instructed the family to give a word gift to each family member by writing a special word beside each person's name. When everyone had finished, we went around the table and each person told out loud the word gift they had written for each person. It was a holy moment!

In Anna's creativity, she added *Twin #1* and *Twin #2* at the bottom of the page because we were all excited that our son and his wife were expecting twins in October of 1998. Caroline, the middle daughter, in her sensitivity, wrote the word *hopeful* by both *Twin #1* and *Twin #2*. I cried. Then Bop prayed a blessing, naming quality traits of each person at the table, and a special blessing on the expected twins and their parents. This birthday breakfast became an altar of thanksgiving, focusing a family on gratitude. The twins, a boy and a girl, arrived safely September 29, 1998.

THE PLACE OF THE FAMILY ALTAR

Building an altar before God in the home unites and strengthens the family in a way that nothing else can do. For years one denomination used this slogan: "The family that prays together stays together."

Whether worshiping together in church or in the home, families make a statement about themselves when they choose to worship God as a family.

The place of family altar can be rather simple: wherever the family meets frequently. The place can and should vary. But the habit of worshiping must not vary, for it needs to be consistent and regular. Family altar simply means the family takes time to celebrate their commitment to God by planning consistent time together to pray and read God's word.

Following are some suggestions and examples as to where to have family altar.

Fluffy pillows and down comforters make for soft cuddling and opportune time for nightly prayer rituals. As tiny babies, my grand girls were rocked and sung to sleep by their father every night until they were big enough to sing with him "Jesus Loves Me" and "Hush Little Baby, Don't You Cry." Nighttime prayers, along with Bible stories or chapter books, give way to words of love and comfort as children prepare for sleep.

I know one family who allows each child to choose two books each evening, and one of the two must be a Bible story. This is great reinforcement to what they get in Sunday school. So many of the Bible stories teach moral truths by which to live; reading and rereading them instills truth into their hearts . . . and don't . . . skip . . . words!

Families of my generation gathered around tables, at home, at our grandparents' homes, at friends' homes. More than food was shared. Life stories were told and retold. God's stories were told. Laughter and tears mixed together. If you grew up in a kitchen-table home, you know that is where everything is dumped. Back packs after school . . . sports bags . . . groceries from the market . . . books from the library . . . Bibles and Sunday school lesson books . . . heartaches . . . relationship problems. How about turning that table into an altar? Oh, I know it doesn't look like an altar most of the time, but if life is shared around the table and covered with love, concern, kindness, prayer and Bible verses, that turns a dumped-on table into an altar.

Kitchen tables become an altar as:

- A mother leans over a coloring child, and says, "Oh, darling, what an artist you are! I thank God for your gift with colors."

- A wife leans down with a gentle hug as the husband writes checks to pay bills, and she whispers, "I really thank God for your gifts and strengths that provide for our family."

- An older sister affirms a little sister as she does her homework.

- A friend listens over coffee to your heartbreak and prays for you.

In this process people have used His name and expressed a blessing or thanksgiving—a kitchen table has become an altar.

Seemingly, the art of eating together as a family is about to be lost! Family experts tell us that the only night the entire American family is together today . . . is Sunday night! After eating and while sitting around the table can be a great time for family night and family worship. It can be preparation to begin another week. Perhaps the family can miss Sunday evening church every so often to get things ready in advance and not feel so rushed. This, of course, would eliminate most church staff families!

My daughter's family has a family night dinner with special dishes and candles; they use this time to discuss responsibilities related to their chores . . . and their allowances. This is a perfect time to share prayer requests for each other and close with sentence prayers.

When our children were growing up, we had family night on Friday. Each family member had the privilege of choosing the activity for that evening (bowling was my least favorite), planning and helping prepare the meal for the event, setting and clearing the table, or occasionally selecting a restaurant, with everyone sharing in the table conversation.

For a period of time, the family member who told the funniest story from their week received the dollar that was placed on the refrigerator with a magnet. This little item helped insure table conversation. This meal was an excellent time to discuss issues that affected our family, school, and community. On these evenings, we planned worship after the evening's event. Most family events are opportunities for altar times, building family unity in Christ, and building family memories.

I am acquainted with families that celebrate family altar each mealtime in the month of December. As Christmas cards arrive, one card is selected from the card basket and the note or name of the sender is read. The blessing always includes the family or friend who sent the card. What a wonderful way to be a blessing to others. This table altar can be extended as long as there are cards and families for which to pray.

One year as our family set out our goals for the upcoming year, we asked two other families with the same configuration as ours if they would enter into a prayer covenant with us for one year. The parents prayed for the mother and father, and the children prayed for each other. These three families all lived in different cities, so calls and letters furnished us with prayer requests and answers. If I were doing this today, I would connect with aunts, uncles, and cousins . . . by e-mail, which is another great way to keep families connected. E-mail can become an ongoing altar, you might say.

Bob and I have always dedicated each of our homes to the Lord. You see, the home does not belong to us . . . it belongs to Sun Bank! We are to be stewards of the home and use it in such a way that it is a blessing to the Father.

When we moved into our home in West Palm Beach, where Bob was to teach at Palm Beach Atlantic College, we bought an old home near the Intercoastal Waterway. We pulled up the carpet and found someone to sand the beautiful hardwood floors. As we went in and out to check on the progress, what a delight to discover someone was singing the gospel. Our floor finisher was singing praises at the top of his lungs. Sometimes, he would stop singing and start praying. I happened to be in the room that was soon to be my office. I was unpacking boxes as he was putting the finishing touches on the dining room floor and singing. He stopped singing and began to pray. I stopped to listen.

"Father, I consecrate this dining room floor to you. I've done my best and I've used my gifts, but now I consecrate these floors to You and pray that everybody who comes in Bob and Esther's home and sits around their table will feel the love of God."

Then he prayed over the living room, the bedroom, and every other room in the house. I was standing in my office with tears running down my face, saying to the Lord, *We always dedicate our home to You, but I've never had anyone consecrate our home even before we moved in.* He stopped praying and moved out of the kitchen and through the garage. I knew he was coming to the front door, and I did not know whether to tell him I'd been to the worship service or not, but it was so obvious as the tears ran down my face. I said, "Oh. Sir! Bob and I thank you for consecrating our home to the Lord." An altar of thanksgiving!

Any room in your home can be an altar before the Lord. If it is true that we have lost that influence on the home, perhaps we should consider making the kitchen or dining table once more the center of family gatherings where the Word, laughter, tears, conversations, and struggles are all accepted, graced, prayed over, and given to the Father for His ever watchful care.

I remember a time when our children were in grade school and our TV was broken. It was several weeks before the TV was returned to our family room. Upon its return, our son, David, said, "I wish the TV was still broken, 'cause we talked to each other more often and played games together." That was amazing insight from a child who watched limited TV, but it was a profound truth. Please hear my heart. It is not so much the place where family altar takes place, it is . . . that it takes place. It can be any place.

Turning everyday events into sacred moments is made simpler when we take advantage of the seasons of the year for occasions of celebration.

Use the seasons as times of celebration for the gifts and opportunities of that season. Check out some library books related to Thanksgiving, Christmas, and Easter. Look for creative ways to involve the family in planning worship celebrations. With the children, make a Christmas month calendar, from December 1 till December 25. This could be very elaborate . . . with homemade Christmas items to place in each pocket of the tree on the banner . . . or simple crayon-colored items to help the children count down the days from December 1 to Christmas Day.

Plan a family evening in November to make the banner and items to be placed in every pocket. Mom will have to gather the material prior to the planned evening. Let all family members have a part in the preparation. Make a big event of hanging the banner! Tell the children they will take turns each day till the twenty-fifth . . . daily taking an item from the pocket and placing it on the tree. After completing the project, gather the children around a big fire in the fireplace (if available) and pop popcorn, snuggle under a favorite quilt or blanket, and have the daddy read part of the Christmas story. Have the mother pray a blessing for each child by name, thanking God they can celebrate Jesus' birthday together. An altar indeed!

Depending on the ages of the children, have a video night, choosing videos that teach family values. After viewing the video, have a family dialogue about the truth taught. Relate this to a recent family situation if possible. Open the Word of God as often as you can to teach your children reliance on God's promises and principles. Close the evening with prayer time—always giving the children an opportunity to pray. Family worship—in the family room!

Retreats are very popular today. When our children were in grade school, my parents were to come for the Christmas holidays. Serving as a campus minister at that time and working with college students on retreats, I thought, *Why not plan a family retreat that would take place in the family room on special evenings after dinner?* Because my parents lived in either Canada, California, or Texas, and both families were in ministry, our children had not been around them much.

My purpose was to help my children and their grandparents get better acquainted with each other and perhaps discover a new way to look at Christmas. We were new to the neighborhood that year, and I wanted to get to know our neighbors. The children and I prepared goody baskets for all the neighbors. Yes, the kitchen was a mess, but I was teaching values and virtues that last a lifetime.

We began the week by Christmas caroling to all the neighbors on Monday. There we were—parents, grandparents, and children—singing on the doorsteps of our neighbors. Quickly, the lights would come on and the family would appear at the door. They seemed delighted as we sang and wished them a Merry Christmas, leaving our gift of goodies. We noticed that even Tabatha, our family kitten, was with us, following along right behind. Caroling gave us a chance to meet our neighbors and leave the fragrance of Christ as we sang the message of Christ's birth. The next year we were asked if we would carol again.

Tuesday night I assigned parts of the Christmas story to the children and grandparents. They were instructed to go to separate rooms, read the portion of the Luke 2 Scripture on the card I had prepared for them, and prepare a skit to present to the whole family. David, age ten, and his grandfather were to pretend they were the innkeeper and his son—who was standing just outside the manger and saw the baby and his mother—and tell us the story through the eyes of the little boy.

Melody, age thirteen, and her grandmother were to retell the story of Mary—explaining to her mother that she was to have the baby Jesus. Bob and I told the story through the eyes of the shepherds. I wish I had put this worship time on tape, but there were no VCRs in those days! I would certainly treasure the memory of that sweet time together.

Wednesday night we shared family traditions from both my parents' growing-up homes. My parents' childhoods and my childhood took place in Canada, so that made it interesting for my children. In winter, my dad took the hose and watered down the garden till it froze to make a skating rink. They loved hearing their parents' stories of celebrating Christmas in the *olden* days! If you ever tell your children stories of your growing-up days, they will beg to have you tell them over and over. Think of this as passing on your heritage.

Thursday night we prepared a basket and gifts for a needy family in our city, teaching our children to share what we had been given. My daughter now has three girls of her own, and this is one of their Christmas family traditions. They bake, shop, and wrap gifts together, sharing the love of Christ with other families.

My own memory is that our Christmas family retreat was very meaningful to our small family and took place mostly in our family room. It did take work and preparation . . . with much help from the children.

The more we let our children help with family altar, the more meaningful it became to them. Remember, an altar helps the family focus no matter where you choose to celebrate in worship.

THE PLAN FOR A FAMILY ALTAR

Family altar will take planning. In fact, to have a successful altar, it must be put on the family calendar along with other important dates. Having a successful altar takes planning. Someone has to do the behind-the-scenes stuff.

Don't be discouraged if you have never done this before and are just now thinking about beginning. Call the family together and share with them that you want to be obedient to God in leading your family in scriptural truth. You may have to say that you are sorry that as a family you have not done this in your home before but that you and the family are choosing to begin today. Little children will accept it. Teens may not like it, but they will most likely feel safe and loved by your effort to begin an altar time.

Anytime is a good time to start. Start slow. Most families could not do family altar today the way my parents did for the obvious reasons that family schedules today are more hectic and families seldom eat together around the table. If you carefully plan to do worship twice a month, you will probably do it twice a month. Family altar does not have to mean that all family members are present every time. It may be a mother-son afternoon of shopping and a quiet dinner together . . . a father-daughter planned time with the intention of sharing meaningful life conversations and a promise of prayer about ideas discussed . . . prayer at your children's bedside later that night.

When our daughter got married, I planned way ahead to have a time with her by myself on the night of the rehearsal dinner. We got home in the afternoon and piled onto her bed and I read one of her favorite bedtime stories to her, *The Velveteen Rabbit*. Then we talked about the fact that she was starting her own home and, at the same time, would be getting a whole new family on her husband's side and what all that would come to mean. We had a good cry and a laugh together. I told her, "The bottom line is that you continue to become real with yourself and family; that's a good rule to live by and it will please the Father." Then we prayed together.

When our son got married, Bob and I wanted to give him a significant gift of love; we came up with the idea to write our long-time friends with whom we'd grown through our years of marriage (many of whom had a great impact on our marriage and ministry), and ask them to write words of wisdom and counsel about marriage to our son. Many of these special friends had watched David grow and mature to manhood and had prayed with us through the years as we raised our family. Their words of wisdom was our way to give a blessing to our son and his new bride.

When life boils down to the bottom line, family and friends are what matter. They are the stuff of treasured moments . . . holy moments . . . lasting memories.

Family altar is looking for opportunities to see eternal significance in everyday matters. *Family altar* is seeing the sacred in the ordinary, and catching the moment.

If your purpose is to have family altar, begin by setting goals and by making plans to carry out those goals.

• Check the family calendar, find a spot, and mark it "Family."

- Go to the bookstore and purchase age-appropriate family worship idea books.
- Gather needed materials.
- Jot down an order of events:

  Bible story

  Bible truth or memory verse to learn

  Questions

  Prayer time

- Look ahead for worship opportunities, such as dedication of your home, Thanksgiving worship, special dinner with close friends, Christmas events, or outdoor worship. These will take careful planning and preparation. Plan ahead so it won't overwhelm at the last minute.

Plan family altar around events such as after church on Sunday night. If you don't have Sunday night church, this is a wonderful time to begin. Plan a family dinner, using your best china for your best guests—your family. Share responsibilities with the children in the preparation of the meal and in the planning for family worship time.

As our children grew older, they were given the opportunity to plan the altar time and to lead the family in worship. This is a wonderful way to encourage their gifts and abilities. Special events at church are another opportunity to invite friends over for dessert and end the time by singing around the piano and offering prayers as a blessing for the next week.

When we moved to Jacksonville, Florida, for Bob to become the director of church music for the Florida Baptist Convention, we purposefully chose a smaller home, which meant we did not need all our furniture. We offered the extra furniture to our children. As David and his dad loaded a U-Haul truck and were ready to head back to Louisville, Kentucky, making a drop at his sister's home on the way, we asked them if we could pray over the furniture because it had been a blessing to us, had graced our home, and was shared with many guests. We wanted to pass that blessing along. There we stood in the driveway with David and Colleen. We shared a Scripture and prayed over the furniture and the truck—asking God to bless the furniture in their home and to give them joy and safe travel. An altar of worship in our driveway.

In my childhood, we never left on a trip that my father did not pray and ask for *journeying mercies.* A woman I once met at the airport for a speaking engagement prayed as we got in the car: "Put an angel on every wheel, God—we're out of here!" Off we went, both laughing in God's presence!

THE PRESENCE AT THE ALTAR

Family altar offers opportunity for the family to experience the presence of God in the home. Every altar time will not be holy or even memorable. Only once did Jesus take His disciples to the mount where they saw Moses and Elijah. Peter was so over-whelmed that he wanted to stay. Then Peter and John were so sur-prised by God's voice from heaven affirming His Son that the disciples fell on their faces. What a Holy interruption! Again, this happened only *one* time.

Most of the other times the disciples spent with Jesus were cooking fish at campfires, walking dusty roads, storytelling on hill-sides, and teaching sessions. There are probably times you walked out of worship on Sunday morning and whispered quietly to your mate: "The Spirit was present this morning." But you don't say it every Sunday, do you? All God asks is worship with the proper atti-tude and adoration. *The issue here is not about the altar being holy, but about the heart being humble and obedient to God's commands.*

Since our son David was in the first grade, we have celebrated

Advent in our family. Advent seemed such a natural event for family worship. I bought a book that showed us how to make the wreath and how to select the Scriptures for the four weeks of celebration.

We desired to teach our children the spiritual significance of Advent. The meaning of *Advent* is simply "coming." We looked up the Old Testament prophecy, looked for the fulfillment in the New Testament, and then memorized a Scripture promise of Christ's return. It took time the first year to write out all the memory verses—placing the verses on star symbols with a string attached for placement on a wreath.

When we first started our Advent celebration, the children were only old enough to argue about who lit the candles every night. But they were getting the ritual of it, and I knew they would get the meaning of the laws and precepts of God as the years went by. When we first began Advent, we made the wreath and took time to worship every night. As the children grew, we did Advent on Sundays only.

One year we chose to worship as a family from Advent all the way through Holy Week. After Christmas, David took our Christmas tree, cut off all the branches, and made a cross from the limbs of the tree. He hammered the cross into a block of wood so that it would stand upright. Yes, it looked like a child made it. The nails were sticking up all over the bottom. We used that cross for eighteen years in our home on special worship occasions. It became the center for us and drew us together.

It was our children who taught us in the Lenten season to give up meals so we could give the money to those who were hungry. I'll never forget reading the Scripture to the children during Holy Week. The starlight of the candle seemed to dim as life got darker and darker for Jesus and His disciples that last week. We had put candles around the foot of the cross, and each day in worship we extinguished one candle. We talked on Good Friday about how the disciples must have felt losing their friend. When we got to Saturday's worship time, we listened to a cassette of Keith Miller telling the story of the crucifixion in the first person, as if he were Matthew. We could hear those nails being pounded into the cross, and little David, who was not a Christian at the time, cried out: "Momma! No! Don't let them kill Jesus!"

I said, "Oh, David. He had to die. That's why He came. But, David, Easter morning we will celebrate His resurrection from the grave!" The Christian faith is the only faith that celebrates the risen, living Christ. Alleluia! What a Savior!

After listening to the tape I placed a black cloth shroud over the cross, and we talked about feelings of separation and death. We talked about losing our puppy and how that death felt to us as a family since that was the only death we'd experienced at the time. We were trying to teach how Jesus' friends must have felt losing Him and reveal their wrong thinking that He was going to set up an earthly kingdom.

Early on Easter morning, I got up and lifted the shroud from the cross, replaced the candles with fresh daisies, and put back the black cloth over the cross. I put on the record player, "He Is Alive!," from the musical *Celebrate Life*, "He is alive! He is alive! He is alive!" I ran upstairs into Melody's room, opened her door, and shouted, "Get up! Get up! It's Easter morning! He is alive!" We then went to David's room, saying the same thing, "Get up! Get up! It's Easter morning! He is alive!" We got to Papa's room last, and we burst in with the same words, "Get up! Get up! It's Easter morning! He is alive!"

We all ran down to the den, and David lifted off that shroud and saw the daisies. He was wide-eyed with surprise, and the four of us sat on the floor of that Birmingham home singing together through our tears, "He is alive! He is alive!" You know what? We really didn't need to go to big church that Sunday. We had already had big church. But, my friends, when you make an altar in your home, it draws you back to the body of Christ to worship before Holy God!

1. Read John 4:20–24.

2. Where does Jesus say the place of worship is?

3. Write the word of instruction given in these Scriptures:
   • Genesis 22:5

   • Deuteronomy 6:13

   • 2 Chronicles 29:28

4. Married or single, do you have family altar in your home?

5. Describe your own quiet time of worship.

6. If you desire to begin family altar, list your goals.

MORE SPLASHING: Visit a local Christian bookstore and browse through the Family or Worship Books section. Carefully select age-appropriate books to help you build a family altar.

1. Rabbi Solomon Granzfried, trans. Hyman E. Goldin, "Code of Jewish Law" (New York: Hebrew Publishing, 1993) Code IV, 47.

7

SHARING
THE DIPPER

Throughout His ministry, Jesus would ask people for certain things He needed. At the same time He would engage them in conversation, which often led to His being able to minister to them. On one occasion He asked a man for a pitcher of water and a room, and He proceeded to serve His disciples the Last Supper. We cannot forget that He asked His disciples to ask a man for the use of his donkey for His triumphant entry into Jerusalem as the Servant king!

Such was the case that hot afternoon at the Samaritan well, when He asked the woman for a drink. She was amazed—not only that He spoke to her, but also that He did not have something with which to dip the water from the well. Because He asked her to serve Him the water, He was then able to offer her His life-giving water. Many people from her village came to know Him as their personal Savior because He and the woman had shared a dipper of water that became for her the living water. What a splash that made!

On another occasion near the end of His earthly ministry, Jesus sat with His disciples and was about to share their last meal together. He noticed that no one had taken care of the basic necessity of hospitality for that day and age: washing the guests' feet. After an experience of speaking in Cairo, Egypt, I have a whole new appreciation for the hospitable practice of washing your guest's feet, dusty and dirty from road travel. Everywhere we walked the dust made itself at home on our feet and clothing. Several times during my stay I thought, *How nice it would be to have a foot bath!*

If the cross is a sign of submission, then the towel must be the sign of servanthood. Jesus set the example for us to follow. He picked up a towel, poured water in a basin . . . and modeled a lifestyle for you and me.

"Just as the Son of Man did not come to be served, but to serve, and to give His life for a ransom for many" (Matt. 20:28).

Richard Foster, in his book *Celebration of Discipline*, invites his readers to "Live simply, so others may simply live." What a challenge to the Christian culture.

We live in a culture that says *get*, and Jesus says *give*.

Our culture says *be* yourself and Jesus says *deny* yourself.

Our culture says *find* yourself and Jesus says *lose* yourself.

I recently heard a bank advertisement announcing a loan program. The announcer said these astounding words: "It makes sense to have it, even if you don't need it."

I thought to myself, *Only in America would anyone believe such a lie.* We might ask ourselves this question: "When is enough enough?" We must choose to live as Great Commission Christians—making a difference in our world for the sake of Christ. My challenge for you in this chapter is to live intentionally—sharing the dipper.

Some years ago, I was invited to write an article on the subject of servanthood. In my preparation, I called a missionary friend in South Florida for an interview. After our opening greetings, I said: "John, tell me what you do that I can share with teenagers that will inspire them to touch their world with Christ's love?" He laughed, thought a moment, and then told me the following story.

When Barbara and I arrived in South Florida, it was evident that we needed to begin some kind of ministry to the migrant farm workers and their families. The children needed food and proper clothing as well as help with school lessons. I called a group of pastors together in the neighborhood and presented the needs of this people group and asked for their help. Many were eager to help. They went back to their congregations and presented the plan.

They asked for teachers to volunteer after school and in the evening to tutor these children. They asked for families in their churches to gather food and clothing to share with the migrant children. They requested toys and school supplies. They also asked for volunteers to do children's programs on Saturday mornings. It all seemed overwhelming—until it was given to the women-on-mission group, who organized it beautifully and carried out the plans. We could always count on the women to have a heart for those in need.

Some months later, a building was secured and stocked with all necessary supplies, and enough volunteers were ready to assist.

I thought to myself as John gave me the details, *This sounds a lot like the early church!*

Word about the services of the mission center spread by word of mouth among the farm workers. Shortly after the center opened, an old car drove up in front of the mission center. A young woman got out of the car and came into the center, with two small children following.

I sensed John smiling over the phone.

The little fella had diapers hanging down to the ground in need of a change, and the little girl's hair looked like it needed a good brushing. I thought to myself, *Wonder what kind of momma this lady is?* Then I heard God's whisper, *Remember the little ones.*

"Can I help you?"

"Is this the place you get them clothes?"

"Yes, it is."

"What do ya got to do to git some?"

"Just help yourself, lady, but we do have a rule here."

"What kinda rule?"

"Our rule is this: If you have some . . . give some. If you need some . . . take some."

With that comment, the lady helped herself to many items of clothing and food. I cared for the children as she loaded up the supplies. Walking her to the car, I helped her fill out an information card, which would enable the mission center to follow up with the family needs.

Feeling good about his first customer, John was certainly not prepared for a return visit from that first customer two weeks later! The same car pulled up in front of the mission center and the same lady got out of the old car with two bags in her hands—but no children by her side.

She came in the front door, and without even saying hello, she said to me: "You did say the rule was 'if you have some . . . give some,' didn't you?"

"Yes," John responded, with surprise.

"Well," she said. "Here!"

Then she thrust into my hands two brown grocery sacks full of soiled baby clothes, smiled at me, turned, and walked away.

I will never forget John's words to me.

She heard the good news! 'If you have some . . . give some.'
She heard, and in her poverty, she gave what she had.

Wow! As I hung up the phone, I kept thinking of the rule about giving and taking and thought it sounded like a good definition of the body of Christ—and not only that, I was quite certain Jesus had said those very words, so I began flipping through my Bible in search of this truth. Notice how close it is to Luke 9:24: "For whoever wishes to save his life shall lose it, but whoever loses his life for My sake, he is the one who will save it.

Look at the role model Jesus lived before us. His challenge to the disciples—and to us in Matthew, chapters 5, 6, and 7—was so radical in a culture bound by rules and looking out for number one. Even His chosen disciples argued over who would be first and have the seat of honor when the kingdom is established! Think about it. This is not too different from the way we live in today's world, is it? The mother of the sons of Zebedee even gets into the picture and says to Jesus: "Command that in Your kingdom, these two sons of mine may sit, one on Your right and one on Your left" (Matt. 20:21).

Jesus tells that pushy mom—and the disciples—that it is His Father who makes that choice. When the other disciples become indignant, Jesus calls them to Himself for one more powerful lesson.

"You know that the rulers of the Gentiles lord it over them, and their great men exercise authority over them. It is not so among you [what a powerful statement about being a disciple], but whoever wishes to become great among you shall be your servant, and whoever wishes to be first among you shall be your slave; just as the Son of Man did not come to be served, but to serve, and to give His life a ransom for many." (Matt. 20:25–28)

These words haunt my life: *Not so among you*. What might the world look like if we who call ourselves Christians lived by His

SPLASH THE LIVING WATER

words: *Not so among you.* If we learned to live not always wanting first place—the highest honor, the esteem—but were willing, like Paul, to be a doormat for Christ? I wonder . . .

Not only did Jesus say He came to serve and not to be served, but He lived out that truth as He encountered the chosen disciples.

DOUG SULLIVAN TAUGHT ME TO STOOP

As you recall from an earlier chapter, I served as the campus minister for Samford University, Birmingham, Alabama, in the seventies. My professor/husband and I enjoyed a wonderful nine years working with those delightful students. Strong student leaders made a deep impact on our lives. They continue to do so even to this day in their leadership positions throughout the U.S. and even unto the uttermost parts of the world.

I remember well the day these two young men hit the campus by storm. They were tall, good looking, and twin brothers—Doug and Don Sullivan. The time came for Campus Ministry elections in Doug's senior year, he was elected president of Campus Ministries! The members of Campus Ministries Council were sitting around the conference table one afternoon going over the last details for the upcoming before-school campus retreat. Business was completed, prayer time was over, and Doug asked me if he could say a word to the council. "Of course," I responded. He then asked if the council members would get comfortable on the floor right outside in the office reception area. He dimmed the lights and left the room.

In a matter of minutes, he walked back through the door, carrying a basin of water, with a towel draped over his shoulders. He sat down in the middle of the group—all six feet of him—with a grin on his face as wide as he was tall!

He said to us: "This year, as your president, I want to be your servant. I don't want to stand before you—but beside you. I want to serve you in such a way that you will be able to do your work on this council by serving the students on campus." Then he opened his Bible and read the Scripture John 13. "As your leader, I want to make a covenant with you to be your servant, and I would like the privilege of washing your feet."

I gasped, thinking, *What a great idea! Wish I'd thought of that!* My next thought was just like that of Peter, *Not me, Lord!*

Quietly, Doug began making his way around the circle of leaders, taking off their shoes and socks amid awesome stillness, washing, and drying feet. He looked into the eyes of each person and said: "I want to be your servant. Let me wash your feet." The closer he got to me, the more I pulled my legs up under my skirt, not willing to allow this student to wash my feet. Quickly, the Spirit got my attention. This was not about my not wanting this—it was about his willingness to do it.

Wow! Have you ever had your feet washed? It is both humbling and freeing. When Doug got to me, he must have sensed my shy resistance. Looking deep into my heart, he simply said, "Mrs. B, I want to serve you, too. May I wash your feet?" I nodded, as tears slowly began to spill from my heart through my eyes.

You would not be surprised at all if I told you campus ministry had a very good year.

I will always be grateful for that lesson in bending down to serve. My life was deeply changed by those generations of students who, through their lives, challenged my ministry.

Chuck Swindoll says, "Love that looks upward is worship. Love that looks outward is adoration. Love that stoops is grace."

Again the Master teacher shows us the way:

- He stooped—to pick up little children to bless them.

- He stooped—toward Thomas, extending his nail-scarred hands.

- He stooped—to write in the sand, forgiving a sinful woman.

- He stooped—to wipe embarrassment from Peter's denial.

- He stooped—to agonize in prayer in a garden.

- He stooped—to a cruel death on a cross, inviting all to eternal life.

He lived a life in *amazing grace*—so amazing that, for the most part, we still don't get it. How do I know? We still find it impossible to live consistently by the Sermon on the Mount!

Let me share more stories of some who have attempted to embrace a servant lifestyle.

MYRTLE HASH TAUGHT ME TO STOOP

Myrtle Hash taught me to stoop. I was serving as mission leader of our women's mission group in the church we attended in Atlanta, Georgia. Several weeks before Thanksgiving, a call came to me from the Salvation Army—asking if our women would be willing to cook some turkeys to feed the homeless. I said I thought we could and would check on it and get back to them. The person also said that the Salvation Army would bring the turkeys to our church and return to pick them up after they were cooked. All we had to do was to get them roasted! I began calling the women and found wonderful willingness to do this task.

I was to speak to one of our group meetings with the older women of the church, and while there, I shared the request of the Salvation Army. I could see most of them nodding their heads in agreement—all but Myrtle Hash, who was seventy years young. Her beautiful white head was shaking a big, emphatic no! Before I could think of what to say in this situation, she said, "Not me! I won't cook a turkey . . . but I will go to the Salvation Army and feed the hungry on Thanksgiving." I'm thinking, *I'm the leader! I'm supposed to think like that!* So I immediately said: "And I'll go with you!" She said playfully, "And I'll see to that." She called several times to remind me of my promise!

I made arrangements with my married daughter so we could eat our Thanksgiving dinner later in the day. Thanksgiving morning arrived, and I went upstairs to wake our college-age son to tell him he did not have to get up—he could sleep in since we would eat later that day. (You see—he'd wakened me up so much during his young life that I thought it was fair to wake him!) I told him I was going to the Salvation Army to feed the homeless. As I began to walk out of his room, I heard him say: "Way to go, Mom!" As I left the room, I heard him yell, "Mom, can I go with you?"

"I'm leaving in five minutes," I said. "If you can be in the car in that time!" I knew full well that he had never taken a five-minute shower in his life! But he did indeed join me—and off we went to pick up Myrtle Hash.

I must confess to you I had never done anything like this before in my life, so I thought it would be good to dress down for the assignment—only to discover when I got there, I was still dressed up!

Being a rather reserved person, I was uncomfortable seeing the long lines of people spilling outside the building and waiting to be fed a Thanksgiving dinner. There were young mothers with little ones . . . wanting formula, diapers, and a hot meal . . . in my very city! There were older people . . . living with poverty, waiting for someone to show amazing grace to them. I found the plastic utensils and began folding napkins around the knives and forks, keeping my back to those young mothers. Myrtle and David went right to the kitchen to begin preparing to serve the food. Then a terrible thing happened! I ran out of utentils, and just about the same time I heard my name called out . . . loud enough for everyone in the shelter to hear it! I followed the sound and saw Myrtle, her hands on her hips, staring me down. "Are you serving any food?

"Well, I was fixing the plastic tableware."

"And is that what you came to do? Get in here and serve the food."

She is my elder, so I obeyed! She shoved a tray of food into my hands and said, "Go!" I walked into the eating area and quickly put the tray down on the table without making any eye contact with the person seated there. You see, I hadn't learned about stooping yet. I hurried back to the kitchen. She handed me yet another tray and asked me, "Well, what did they say?"

"I'm supposed to *talk* to them?"

"Esther! Why did you come here? Serve them . . . and talk to them!" she commanded as she shoved another tray into my hands. This time I allowed myself to look around and see the many faces of need. I set the tray down in front of a man whose eyes showed little hope and whose knurled hands told me his story. As I looked into his eyes, I said, "Sir, I'm glad you came here today."

He reached over, put his hands on mine, and said: "Lady, I'm glad you came today!"

After several hours of hard—but rewarding—work, David and I drove home in silence . . . each in our own thoughts with Kodak memories of the people we had met that morning. Thank you, Myrtle, for teaching me: If you have some . . . give some. If you need some . . . take some. Love that stoops is grace!

DR. BOB HAMBLIN TAUGHT ME TO STOOP

Dr. Bob Hamblin was my supervisor when I was on the evangelism staff of the Southern Baptist Home Mission Board (now the North American Mission Board). He told me this story about an experience a number of years ago with the Billy Graham Itinerate Evangelism Conference in Amsterdam, Holland.

Dr. Graham had invited a large number of American ministers to attend this conference. As they gathered to hear his words, Dr. Graham told the Americans that, as they had noticed, he had not invited them to be on the platform as speakers . . . but he desired for them to serve the men and women from the third-world countries who had come to this conference for evangelism training. He continued to tell the ministers they were to do the menial things for the conference, such as man the registration booth, run the welcome center, operate the lost and found, serve in the cafeteria lines. In other words, he wanted them to be ministers and servants to their brothers and sisters from around the world.

Dr. Hamblin later said to me, "I wondered if Dr. Graham knew who I was! I was vice president of the evangelism section of the Home Mission Board of the Southern Baptist Convention! Why, I had spoken in some powerful pulpits in America."

As the week progressed, the Americans found themselves doing exactly what Dr. Graham had asked them to do . . . being servants. As Dr. Hamblin continued his story, he said, "As Ruth and I served in the food line, we watched the men and women from the third-world countries put sandwiches in each of their pockets. I suppose they thought this might be their food for the week . . . or perhaps they were just hungry. I told my wife that we would go across the street to McDonald's so there will be plenty of food left for them."

At the end of the week, Dr. Graham again called the American ministers together. This time he asked them to go back to their hotels, take out a suit of clothing, and be prepared to bring it to the altar to give to a third-world brother in the final service of the conference. When Bob and Ruth got back to their hotel, Bob said he was thinking in his heart, *I wonder if Dr. Graham knows where I buy my clothes?*

He told me that his heart won out. The last day when the altar call was given, he and his wife made their way to the altar and laid down one of his suits. He also laid down a shirt, a tie, a pair of shoes, and socks. His wife also laid down one of her dresses. His next words struck my heart: "For the first time in my life, I understood *real power!*" The heavenly Father must have smiled over the altar that day, but surely all of heaven applauded for every bent knee, rejoicing as the family of God served each other.

I was in Amsterdam speaking some years ago and told this story in my message, only to be surprised again by God. A minister came to me and said he had taken some of the clothes from that altar service, had worn them awhile, and then had given them away to another brother in need!

If you have some . . . give some. If you need some . . . take some. Love that stoops is grace!

DR. SHIRLEY WILLIAMS TAUGHT ME TO STOOP

One day the phone rang, interrupting my thoughts. The voice was that of Dr. Shirley Williams, director of student ministries for the Missouri Baptist Convention. I quickly remembered that I was to be the speaker in the fall student conference the following week.

"Esther, we've canceled the student meeting at Lake Windermere Conference Center."

My first thought was that this might mean I would have a weekend at home with my husband, but her next words pierced my heart.

"We've canceled the meeting at the conference center and are moving it into the city of St. Louis. As you know, the rivers have overflowed, and mud is everywhere due to the heavy rains, so we are going to mud out the flood victims."

With my heart in my throat, I said, "Yes, the church is going to be the church."

Shirley asked if I still wanted to come to the meeting.

"Absolutely, but only if you will let me work alongside the students."

She then told me the clothing I'd need and the necessary shots I would have to get to protect me. She said that she would supply firemen's rubber boots!

I knew the theme for the meeting was "It's Your Serve!" How like God to set that theme way before the student meeting happened and right when St. Louis needed to see the stooping love of Christians. We began Friday night with an opening celebration . . . and in the closing of that celebration time, each student was given a white golf towel, which had written on it these words: *Towels and Basins.*

Saturday morning, the more than six hundred students were sent out in teams all over St. Louis—with much help from the inner-city missionaries—to mud out houses, feed the hungry in food lines, unload trucks, and organize supplies in a warehouse. I quietly slipped into the back of a van with about fourteen students. They did not recognize me in my fireman's clothes. I worked beside those young people and mudded out a small African-American church and helped to replace dry wall. I watched and listened carefully. The students *sang* the whole time they worked. As we left that church, a number of the church members gathered around and prayed over us.

Our next assignment was a large church. The sanctuary was undamaged, but the basement was in terrible shape. When I looked at the mess down there, my heart sank, wondering what we could possibly do to make a difference. Again the students sang as they mudded out rooms . . . cleaned out trash . . . and painted rooms. Our lunch arrived courtesy of the Baptist Men's Mission Disaster Team van. We blessed the food, and no one said a word about the sandwiches without fixings and sodas without ice!

After finishing up both churches, our leader sent us out in pairs to find neighbors who might need help, instructing us to share Christ with the people we would meet. In no time, everyone had come back to the church, because we could not find anyone close that needed us, until two young boys riding bikes through the flooded intersection pointed us toward a home across the road. We formed a human chain and walked through the water.

An older gentleman was sitting on the steps of the shell of what was once his home and office. Leon Ray had been a photographer in the U.S. Army, and in retirement he still had a studio. We asked if we could help. He shrugged his shoulders. Debris from the flood's destruction was piled outside his home—higher than the roof. He insisted the city government would get to it next week. We insisted on cleaning it up ourselves.

I worked with those students as they sang and sorted that pile of trash. They filled two truck-sized dumpsters with the remnants of Leon Ray's home. As I worked alongside them, the Spirit whispered, *Tell him why you came to help.* I walked over to the step and sat down. After introductions, he told me his wife was not well and that this tragedy put her in bad shape. His voice was tearful as he told of his travels with the government and all the dignitaries whose pictures he had taken. "It's all lost now," he said.

"Mr. Ray, do you know why these students have come today?"

"I think so," he answered quietly.

"They have come in response to a need in the community because of their personal relationship to Jesus Christ."

He smiled for the first time. He told me that he knew Christ. I told him about the student conference and about the more than six hundred students who had spread all throughout St. Louis that day—getting their towels dirty serving Christ. I went back to work and noticed that one by one, the students began to go over and sit by Leon to visit with him.

We were almost to the bottom of the pile of soggy rubbish when I pulled out a Bible with a mother-of-pearl cover, which was still in perfect condition and completely dry. I rushed over to Leon and said, "Look what I found!" I put the Bible in his hands. He smiled a second time.

"This is my wife's Bible, and she will be so happy. Maybe this will help her in this rough time." He held it to his heart. I watched as he opened the Bible. Inside the front cover was a baby picture of their only son. He smiled for the third time . . . through tears. I cried, too.

How gracious of God to preserve His word for this family that lost everything. As we left his ruins, we gathered in a circle to pray, but before one of us could begin, Leon asked if he could pray. And pray he did! The students and I walked back across the intersection through the water with spirits that were walking *on* water.

After working all day, Saturday night's celebration service was electric with joy and excitement. We came to the service dirty from mudding out the houses—but with hearts clean and fresh like a mountain stream. In the closing ceremony, I asked the students, "If you are willing to go back to the campuses to serve your fellow students, come to the altar and put your towels on the nails on the cross." I stepped away from the podium and was amazed at what I saw and heard. Students began tearing their towels in half . . . wanting to keep a reminder of that experience . . . and then brought the other half to the cross. What a picture . . . a cross covered in torn white towels! I owe a great debt of gratitude to those Missouri students because they allowed me to serve with them. Because of students willing to be servants, I have great hope for our nation.

If you have some . . . give some. If you need some . . . take some. Love that stoops is grace!

FRAZIER MEMORIAL TAUGHT ME TO STOOP

Frazier Memorial United Methodist Church in Montgomery, Alabama, is a true servant church. Their pastor, John Ed Mathison, has a passion for freeing the laity to do the work of the ministry. The youth group of the church decided that they were spiritually dead and needed a revival. So they began by having a funeral and burying their old program; then they began to build what they thought God desired for them. Think of other churches that might need to do this with a variety of programs! We might have a lot of funerals.

Their pastor's passion for hands-on missions was the flame that sent these young people out to minister in their own community. I heard John Ed tell what their youth group did when the state fair came to Montgomery. With a new vision for ministry, the young people got together with their leaders and planned a first-class welcome banquet for the circus workers. They received permission and set the time to have the event in one of the circus tents. The tables were set with the best dishes and glasses available . . . and fresh flowers were on every table. The circus workers, according to their custom, each brought their own eating utensils under their arms.

The young people planned and presented a short program for the workers. The youth expressed gratitude to them for coming to make their state fair a fun and safe place to be.

Then they presented a long-stemmed rose to each circus worker. Some acted surprised. Some wept. Some expressed thanks, saying nothing like that had ever happened to them before. The management of the state fair told the church, "We will never forget Montgomery, Alabama."

If you have some . . . give some. If you need some . . . take some. Love that stoops is grace!

KARLA WORLEY TAUGHT ME TO STOOP

My friend Karla Worley and I were talking about our gardening habits and the joys that come to us because of our gardening. She told me she belongs to a garden group in her church called Yard Angels. I told her that I chose not to take that time to be involved in a group because I just liked to putter alone or with Bob helping me work my small garden.

"Oh, we're not the usual garden club. We do ministry through our gardens."

"Tell me more."

"Well, first of all, when we work in anyone's garden we always leave behind a watering can with a scroll of Scripture in it: 1 Corinthians 3:7. We do work in each other's, but our primary purpose is to do something for another woman who happens to be overwhelmed with life at the moment. We do edging, trimming, planting, landscaping, pruning, and leaf-raking. We don't just pick flowers, honey, we haul trees! We do have fun together, and one of the byproducts is that as we work together, we talk about our own lives and share the things that overwhelm us at the moment and are able to try and encourage each other."

All this time, I thought my garden was for my joy and solitude, and here was this young woman telling me she used her garden to help others! Then I remembered my best friend, Jo Vaughn, telling me that one of the great joys of gardening is sharing the produce. Gardening takes much stooping. So does serving, and my friend Karla and her garden group understand that. If you have some ... give some. If you need some ... take some. Love that stoops ... is grace!

ROGER AND DIANE MCMURRIN
TAUGHT ME TO STOOP

Bob and I met Roger and Diane McMurrin at the 1997 International Church Music Festival in Bern, Switzerland. Roger had served as a successful minister of music in two large and prestigious churches in Florida and Texas. After the Berlin Wall came down in the former East Germany, Roger was invited to come to Kiev, Ukraine, and lead a choir and orchestra in a performance of *The Messiah*. Imagine the Ukrainian people getting to hear those masterworks for the first time in over seventy years! The trip impacted Roger and Diane in such a way that they knew they had to go back to serve those people. They came home, prayed it through, resigned the position at the church, sold their home, gave away their possessions, and promised God ten years in the Ukraine—in Kiev. We get their monthly newsletter and weep with joy at what God is accomplishing through them.

Not being able to speak the language when they first arrived, they needed an interpreter, and he declared to them up front that he was an atheist and needed no God. Because of their work, the interpreter and the McMurrins were together much of the time in choir and orchestra rehearsals, where Sergei translated as he traveled with them around the city. The McMurrins relied on the faith that the folks back home would help financially with their ministry. Each Sunday, meeting in the rehearsal hall, Roger and Diane fixed gallons of potato salad and fresh cabbage—both staples for the Ukrainian people—to feed those attending the services, which included, of course, the interpreter.

The time came for their first communion service—and Sergei took communion. Roger explained to him again that he must first accept Christ. "I have!"

"When?" Roger inquired. "Was it the Scripture you read?"

The interpreter shook his head "No."

"Was it the books we gave you to read, like C. S. Lewis's *Mere Christianity?*"

"No." He smiled.

"It must have been the rehearsal and concert!"

"No" He shook his head.

"What was it then?" Roger pressed on.

"It was your tears!"

The tears Sergei saw were during that first communion as Roger held the elements and saw so many new Christians from his choir coming forward to take Communion, face after face.

This couple had sold everything . . . left home . . . left family . . . and became servants that stoop through His grace in Kiev, Ukraine. Love that stoops . . . is grace! We might add . . . love that stoops . . . stoops with tears!

I cried at his words, wondering if Christ had seen my servant tears. Pondering Christ's words. "Self-sacrifice is the way, my way, to finding yourself, your true self. What good would it do to get everything you want but lose the real you?" (Matt. 16:26, The Message). Someone has said, "Being a servant is being willing to do the menial tasks day after day, no one noticing and no one saying thanks, but being willing to serve the task for Christ's sake."

If you have some . . . give some. If you need some . . . take some. Love that stoops . . . is grace!

JOHN AND ANN FAULKNER TAUGHT ME TO STOOP

John and Ann Faulkner invited me to go to Kenya, Africa, to teach a women's mission retreat for missionary wives. The setting was in beautiful Brackenhurst . . . high in the mountains.

The first week was a wonderful time of worship and fellowship. After taking a few days break to see one of the magnificent game parks, we packed up and headed back for the second week of retreat. The leaders told me that this retreat would be a different kind of week, that I would notice the missionaries who come from southern Africa are very different. It did not take long to notice. There was much laughter, joy, and fellowship. Living in a war-ravaged arena, where they are often afraid for their own personal and family safety, they seemed to value every moment of life.

Desiring me to experience what it is like to live in remote areas such as they did, they put me in a skit the first night. I was asked to sit in the seat of honor. Then they placed a live chicken in my lap— much to my surprise and to the ladies' delight. It was a gift I was happy to give back.

They gave me an assignment to go to the post office, an assignment they had designed for this part of the program. They had planned all kinds of interruptions, such as they encounter every day in their mission fields, to keep me from getting there. A beggar accosted me by grabbing at my clothes. The women laughed as I whipped off my earrings and gave them to the beggar. Another beggar came at me, and I took off my necklace and gave it to her. They laughed even harder. They were having great sport with me.

The last time a beggar came, I thought about giving my sweater, but it had huge knitted buttons, so I just pulled down my elastic-waisted skirt as if to give it away. (Please know that there were just women in this audience! Besides, I had on a black slip.) The ladies stood to their feet—screaming and clapping their hands in delight. We laughed until we cried. Later that night I thought, *Yes, these ladies are different. What a sweet gift from the Father that each group had the unique fragrance of Christ.*

The day before I was to leave, the women had a time of testimony and thanked me for coming to be with them. It was a humbling experience to be blessed by the body of Christ.

Kathy stood first and said, "I bless God that Esther came, 'cause I haven't laughed in six months . . . but when you pretended to take off your skirt for the beggar, I laughed. When I got back to my room, I cried and laughed with God 'til the healing started to come."

The ladies applauded. You must know a bit of Kathy's personal story. In their first four years of service, they had major sickness in the family and had their home broken into more than once— enough to make anyone forget how to laugh. Earlier in the week, I had shared the story of the Americans giving away their clothes at the Billy Graham meeting. Kathy continued her words and said through her laughter, "And Esther, if you ever decide to give your clothes away, I want that outfit you had on last night—that skirt and sweater." She could not possibly have known that I had just bought that *Carole Little* outfit for the trip.

I stood and looked at her, and my heart spoke these words: "Kathy, I want you to have that outfit!" I sat down, feeling good about my new friend in Christ. I felt such joy. I wasn't even thinking!

After a time of tears and laughter, everyone headed off to lunch in another building. Kathy waited until everyone was gone to speak with me. "I can't take that outfit, but my national pastor and his wife have just had a fire, and she needs clothes. And if you like, I'll give her some of mine."

"Fine!" I said. But inside my heart, all I could see was her pastor's wife's needs—and the fat suitcase I was packing earlier that morning, getting ready to go home that night.

At lunch that day, one of the missionaries said to me that all the tall missionaries had gotten together. "We know what outfits of yours we'd like to have when you decide to get rid of them." Again, my heart felt a deep impression about my suitcase. I went back to the room and unpacked that suitcase, which then left ample room for all the gifts I'd been given opening night from the women of each country (minus the live chicken!). A shelf in my office is now full of memories and gifts from the missionaries in eastern and southern Africa.

When I spoke later that afternoon, I told the group what Kathy had shared with me about her pastor's wife and what God showed me about my suitcase. To their complete surprise, I said, "My clothes are laid out for you at the back of the room. Please help yourself to whatever you need."

Afterward, Kathy came to me and said, "I don't know how to receive very well, and I really would like to have that dress. In the quiet last night, God reminded me that you gave it to me and that I could receive it." I was so happy, telling her that I really wanted her to have it. We hugged. We cried. Kathy left then. I knew how hard it was going to be to say good-bye to the women. Our tears mixed together.

All of a sudden, the room broke out in full laughter and applause as Kathy came into the dining hall with her new dress on—earrings, necklace, and all—and a big name tag that read *Esther Burroughs*. She walked through the room with the grace of a New York model, to the sounds of her sisters' joyful, laughing tears.

If you have some . . . give some. If you need some . . . take some. Love that stoops . . . is grace!

Jesus said in Luke 9:23–24, "Anyone who intends to come with Me has to let Me lead. You're not in the driver's seat—I am! Don't run from suffering; embrace it. Follow Me and I'll show you how. Self-help is no help at all. Self-sacrifice is the way, My way, to finding yourself, your true self. What good would it do to get everything you want and lose the real you?" (The Message).

Being a servant is not popular. It is difficult. It finally killed Mother Teresa.

Being a servant is not easy. It requires humility—and receives little earthly reward.

Being a servant is not entertaining. It is entertaining angels unaware.

Being a servant is not that hard. It is impossible—without the Spirit of Christ.

Prayer, prison, persecution, and power identify the New Testament church. No wonder the early church knew the joy of loving each other and having all things in common.

Do you think that programs, personalities, popularity, and prosperity might identify today's churches?

What if today's church took seriously the Scripture about the poor, the widowed, the homeless, the children, the sick, and the dying?

Is today's church a servant church? Mission agencies say that the average evangelical church today spends ninety-nine cents of every dollar on itself. What if Jesus had said, "I don't do feet?" How would the disciples—then and now—know how He expected us to live? I believe this begins with one person—just one. Don't say the church isn't doing this or that. *You* are the church. You as an individual can serve, making a difference.

If you have some . . . give some. If you need some . . . take some. Love that stoops . . . is grace!

1. Have you ever experienced footwashing? If so, describe your feeling.

2. When and where was the last time you served someone in your family or in the church family? How did that make you feel?

3. Ask God to show you someone in need. Ask Him how you can be a servant in the situation, without your revealing who you are. Write the name of that person below.

4. Our own families may be the most difficult place to be a servant! Watch for ways you can serve your husband/children. Begin seeing yourself as a servant, and begin serving. Use this space to note the ways you serve.

5. Read John 13 again and think about the words of Jesus to His disciples about holiness versus hygiene as they relate to feet washing. What are your thoughts on this matter?

6. Mother Teresa was asked about the many who died and why she continued to serve there. Her reply: "I choose to see Christ in the face of every man and every need." How does this statement make you feel?

MORE SPLASHING: Read Brennan Manning's *The Ragamuffin Gospel* (Sisters, OR: Multnnomah Publishers, 1993).

8

Soaking Up the Interruptions

Jesus loved life! He invited folks in trees to lunch. He witnessed to those who crossed His path. He ate with sinners . . . forgave adulterous women . . . told stories to children . . . turned water to wine . . . and changed lives forever. He was focused!

When Jesus was an older child, He was teaching in the temple—while His worried parents looked for Him. When they found Him, He said simply: "Why is it that you were looking for Me? Did you not know that I had to be in My Father's house?" (Luke 2:49). During His ministry, He said:

> I can do nothing on My own initiative. As I hear, I judge; and My judgment is just, because I do not seek My own will, but the will of Him who sent Me . . . But the witness which I have is greater than that of John; for the works which the Father has given Me to accomplish, the very works that I do, bear witness of Me, that the Father has sent Me (John 5:30, 36).

He ministered to people—with the weight of the world on His

shoulders and the weight of God's love in His heart. His passion was to do what His Father had sent Him to do.

"For high in the mountains, the tiniest brook gave its life to the stream. The streams flowed together and came to the river," says the songwriter, Bonnie Keen. A profound truth, wouldn't you say?

You and I get our life from the river of living water. As we accept the flow from His life to our lives, we become a river . . . flowing out to a dry and barren land. Imagine living in such obedience to God that the flow of His love from my life develops a thirst in someone else for His thirst-quenching water. How, you might ask.

Let us begin by looking at a typical day in the life of Jesus. You and I live and breathe by our notebook organizers and calendars—while Jesus lived each interruption as God's divine appointment. Think about that: living daily to expect an interruption as a divine appointment with God. Regarding circumstances in our lives, we perhaps are quick to say, "What a coincidence." Or, "You won't believe what happened!" Jesus was never surprised by the activity of God. In fact, He said He only did what the Father told Him to do. No wonder He moved with such assurance and authority.

In Chapter 1, I referred to the interruptions in our daily lives and how we can use them to splash the living water. Let's look at the interruptions in the life of Jesus as found in Matthew, chapters 8 and 9. I've called them *divine encounters*.

Jesus climbs a mountain with His disciples and He teaches them in His famous Sermon on the Mount. When He comes down from the mountain, the crowd is following.

Divine encounter 1: Jesus encounters a leper who bows down to worship Him. Jesus puts forth His hand and touches him. Immediately the leprosy is cleaned.

Divine encounter 2: Jesus walks to Capernaum and is interrupted by a centurion who asks Him for the healing of a servant who is critically ill. Jesus embraces this interruption as the centurion explains the situation. Jesus does not need to go to the soldier's home. Jesus needs only to speak a healing word. When He does, the servant is immediately healed and the centurion's faith is increased.

Divine encounter 3: The disciples go to Peter's house where his mother-in-law is sick in bed. Jesus touches her hand and the fever leaves her. She gets up and prepares a meal for them.

Divine encounter 4: Leaving the house, some demon-possessed people scream at Jesus, and He stops and heals them. Then Jesus tells the disciples to get the boat ready to cross the lake.

Divine encounter 5: A scribe interrupts Jesus, expressing a desire to follow Him before Jesus can get to the boat. Can't you just imagine the disciples—waiting anxiously as Jesus takes His time to visit with this man?

Divine encounter 6: Even before Jesus can get in the boat, another would-be follower expresses a desire to follow Him, but only after he can clear up some family matters. Leaving this man with strong words, a tired Jesus finally gets into the boat and immediately falls asleep.

Divine encounter 7: A storm appears. The disciples finally awaken Jesus to save them from perishing. Once awake, He rebukes the storm and the storm stops. (I wish I could have seen the disciples' faces when that happened!)

Divine encounter 8: Arriving at the other side of the lake, Jesus was ready to rest and have a bite to eat . . . but again, He is interrupted, this time by two demon-possessed men who come running toward the boat. He deals with the men and casts the demons into some grazing pigs that charge into the sea and drown.

Divine encounter 9: Perhaps Jesus is still looking to rest, but the whole town comes out. The people are probably upset about losing their pigs, and they demand that Jesus leave their town. Jesus joins the disciples at the boat and they cross back to Capernaum.

Divine encounter 10: Stepping on shore, Jesus notices the

people bringing a paralytic on a mat to him, and notes their great faith. He heals the boy. Some of the scribes interrupt, calling Jesus a blasphemer, which gives Jesus the opportunity to show God's authority. The multitudes are in awe. Not once does Jesus even inquire about the time of day or complain about all the encounters He has experienced.

Divine encounter 11: As Jesus walks on from there, He sees Matthew and invites him to become a disciple.

What a day! What an example! Consider living in the expectancy of divine encounters and interruptions where the Spirit allows the flow of living water to splash out on the people you encounter and to draw others to the well of living water.

His day was full, just like almost any day on your or my personal calendar, except for the healing events . . . maybe.

Here's a typical day for me:

Monday, the morning of my regular prayer group, finds me up early for my quiet time, which may be interrupted by a phone call from my husband about a matter that needs prayer. The prayer group meets from nine till noon. We share a time of laughter, with confession, tears, concern over situations—and much joy and celebration. After a tearful confession, we speak loving words and allow hearts to mend. I believe that's healing!

Next stop perhaps is the frame shop—where I drop off a wedding invitation to be framed as a gift to a special friend from Bob and me. I think of this young woman, and how God allows Bob and me to minister in her life. So I say, "Patrick, this has to be beautiful. I want it to be a prayer blessing for this young couple as they start married life." He smiles and says, "Another blessing from you, hey?"

Then, perhaps, on to the bank to make a deposit. The clerk says to me, "Have a good day!" My response is, "May God bless your day." As I drive from the bank, I express thanks to God for a weekend speaking engagement where the women enriched my life and encouraged my walk with the Father. Because of their gift to me, I am able to give to others.

My next stop is the grocery store. As I go through the checkout lane, I punch the debit card machine button, asking for fifty dollars back in cash. The young clerk, from Haiti, comments on the much-needed rain in Florida. I respond, "It is an answer to prayer, for sure." She smiles widely and nods that she also has prayed for rain to help put out the fires. (At the time of this writing, much of Florida was on fire!) Our hearts have a knowing exchange. As I walk away, I think to myself, *She is a Christian.* I put the groceries in the car and head for home—in the rain.

Groceries put away, I head for a quick nap—due to a long weekend of travel. But before I get to the bedroom, the phone rings. My best friend is full of good news about her family vacation. After forty-five minutes of love, laughter, and joy, we close our phone time by sharing family prayer requests. What would we do without each other's prayers? No wonder Jesus often invited His disciples to pray with Him.

Like Jesus on the boat, I also take a nap. Refreshed and with a fresh cup of coffee, I sit down at my computer to continue writing this book. I have just gotten started when a fax comes with another ministry opportunity, which causes me to give thanks for God's faithfulness in my speaking ministry. I stop to fax the copy to my capable assistant.

I am back to my writing when the doorbell rings. It is a neighbor with whom I had coffee about a week ago. She is bringing me a makeup sample from a new shop in her mall. What a great neighbor! I take another break from my writing to edit a manuscript that is due shortly, and just as I finish that assignment, the graphic artist with whom I am working on a newsletter calls. It is a joy to visit with her because she is so gentle and hears the ideas of my heart as she assists my ministry with her artistic gifts.

Once again, I am at my writing desk and totally unaware of the time when I hear the garage door opening and know that my sweetheart is home. His arrival signals our daily ritual. He always comes into the kitchen, opens his briefcase, and shares all kinds of the good stuff from his day at the office, including e-mail from friends and articles and new books he thinks I will enjoy. I share things from my day. We put on our walking clothes and take off for our daily exercise of walking about three miles together. I cherish this time greatly. It is our time to share with each other about our family, our work, our ideas, and our dreams.

In the conversation, I mention I have just come from the grocery, and as he always does, he asks how much I spent on groceries this trip—and in that split second, I realize I had left the grocery store without the fifty dollars cash! As soon as we get home, I call the store and give the receipt number to the manager. She calls back in ten minutes and tells me that the money is still in the cash drawer. I thank God as I get in the car to make yet another trip to the grocery store. I find the young woman who checked me out, and as I go to her counter, she steps out to hug me (it's a woman thing), and she thanks me for coming back. I say, "I thank you. I sensed you are a Christian, and I'm grateful for your honesty." She grins and in her beautiful accent says, "I am! I am!" Back to my car, I thank God again for this short encounter about prayer that led us to express our faith.

As I begin dinner preparation, the doorbell rings. Tea towel in hand, I answer the door to discover a huge basket of flowers! Bob and I are celebrating our fortieth anniversary this year (August 28, 1998) and he has sent a bouquet of flowers every month since January . . . each bouquet containing exactly forty stems of flowers. He is home, so I can embrace him and express my love for the lovely interruption of his love for me.

After supper, conversation, and a few more phone calls, it's time for bed already!

Does my day sound typical to your day? Well, maybe so—with

or without the flowers. My day is full of interruptions, and some allow me to express my faith and love for Christ. We make a choice about our attitude concerning interruptions. Jesus did, also!

Several years ago, someone gave me the late Oscar Thompson's *Concentric Circles of Concern*. For many years before his death, Dr. Thompson was a professor at Southwestern Baptist Theological Seminary in Fort Worth, Texas. In teaching his students about evangelism, he asked God to show him a way to teach them that would change all of eternity. He then studied Jesus in the New Testament and saw His pattern of relationships. Dr. Thompson taught that sharing Christ was about building and repairing relationships.

Think about it. All of life is about relationships.

Bitter relationships . . .

- A child separated from parents
- Family members angry with each other
- Teenage romance and breaking up with a sweetheart
- Jealousy in a friendship
- Loss of a spouse or parent
- Divorce
- Loss of a job
- Struggles in the church

Sweet relationships . . .

- The joy of loving parents
- Laughter from a true friendship
- That first date
- The wedding day

- Friendships at work
- Birth of a child or a grandchild

Good relationships help us to become all that God desires. Unhealthy relationships produce . . .

- Broken relationships
- Broken homes
- Divided churches
- Weak governments

The book of Acts says that they went from house to house. Andrew went to Peter . . . Phillip to Nathaniel . . . the woman at the well to her city . . . Cornelius to his household . . . the Philippian jailer to his family (and this household included servants as well as family members). It is no different today. When family members come to know the saving grace of the cross, they want to tell others who are dear to them about this miracle in their lives. We make a mistake when we think of evangelism as related only to persons we do not know. Doesn't it make sense to share the Good News first with those you do know and about whom you care?

In his book, Dr. Oscar Thompson provides the seven circles of influence in the lives of every person:

1. Self
2. Immediate family members
3. Relatives
4. Close friends
5. Business associates and neighbors
6. Acquaintances
7. Person X

Did you notice that there are *seven* circles? And that there are *seven* days of the week? Begin the week by praying for yourself, and each day thereafter, move out with a flow of prayer for persons in your circle of concern. You will want to update your list regularly as your circle of influence changes with circumstances. When I began praying over my circles of influence, I listed on a page in my prayer journal the persons in each circle. It is a wonderful way to keep up with your circles!

In Chapter 3, I said that out of the inflow comes the outflow . . . gained from our quiet time of worship with the Father. You have no doubt met people whose lives just seem to flow with the love of God. They are like a river that flows and splashes refreshment on all who walk by. Jesus desires that His love flow out of us . . . touching the world. As Paul says in Ephesians 3:19: "To know the love of Christ which surpasses knowledge; that you may be filled with all the fullness of God" (NKJV). I like *The Message* translation: "You'll be able to take in with all Christians the extravagant dimensions of Christ's love. Reach out and experience the breadth! Test its length! Plumb the depths! Rise to the heights! Live full lives, full in the fullness of God." John 7:37–38 reminds us: "If anyone is thirsty, let him come to me and drink. Rivers of living water will brim up, spill out of the depths of anyone who believes in me this way."

The evidence of the fullness of the presence of the Holy Spirit in our lives is directly related to the outflow. If there is a filling there is going to be a flowing. If there is no outflow, you can be sure there is no filling. Obedience and joy are inextricably joined together. *Obedience*—to take the time with the river, to drink up the riches of Christ Jesus. *Joy*—to take every encounter as if sent by God, to drink from the overflow of the river of life in Christ.

In living in the fullness of God, we are aware of our influence and always look for opportunities that can build bridges to rela-tionships—in times of joy as well as in times of sorrow—which allow us to be that flow of living water. The concept that Thompson shares is so profound, it is very simple.

Do you remember as a child, throwing a rock into a lake and watching the ripple spread out from the center where the rock dropped out of sight? As you continued to throw more rocks, you noticed the circles spreading out and beginning to overlap each other.

That beautiful concept works in personal relationships. As our circles of influence go out, touching other persons in their circles of influence, we can live in the expectancy of what the power of the Holy Spirit will do to draw people to Himself.

In class one day, Dr. Thompson said, "God holds us responsible for every person who comes into our circle of influence." He continued by saying, "Some of them are cantankerous, some of them don't like you, and some of them you don't want to love. They are there for you to love—to meet their needs—to draw them to Jesus. "

"Dr. Thompson," a student named Jim spoke up. "I have all kinds of trouble with that. You don't understand my situation. You grew up in a Christian home. But my father abandoned my mother and me twenty-six-and-a-half years ago. I am twenty-seven years old. I have never seen him. *I do not want to see him!*"

At that intense moment, Dr. Thompson prayed for the wisdom of God. He then wrote his translation of Matthew 6:14–15 on the board. "Because of the love of Jesus and His forgiveness in my life, I must be ready to forgive if I am to be forgiven."

Tears rolled down the cheeks of the student. "What must I do? I do not know where my father is. He may not even be alive."

The class immediately went to prayer. Weeks passed. One morning, Jim came into the class and said, "I have something to say to the class, sir. Last night, I received two phone calls. The first came from my mom, saying that one of my aunts had gone to be with the Lord. I thought she was my mother's sister but learned she was my father's sister. At 11:00, I received a second call, and a voice on the other end said, 'Jim? Son? . . . although I have no right to call you son. But I have heard that you are in the seminary preparing for the ministry. I thought you would like to know that I recently gave my life to Jesus Christ. Can you forgive me for what I have done?'" After a pause, Jim continued, "When I could quit sobbing, we talked. We spent an hour on the phone."

In Chapter 5, we talked about the well of living water (which is the Holy Spirit): "He who believes in Me . . . From his innermost being shall flow [gushing up, springing out, flowing over] rivers of living water" (John 7:38). The flow of the Spirit is like a well that flows with rippling effects on those around us.

I heard my pastor preach recently from the John 4 text, and he gave a wonderful illustration. The pastor invited a staff member to bring an old hand pump, like those used on farms in the thirties, to the platform. He demonstrated pumping the handle and showed us the suction cup, bound by a leather washer. That had to be wet to cause the suction as the handle was pumped, drawing water up from the well and out through the spout. He told this story:

"One of the most unusual messages I've ever seen is related to a hand pump like this one. The message was scribbled on a scrap of wrapping paper that had been folded into a baking-powder can and then had been wired to an old hand pump. That pump offered the only chance of water on a seldom-used trail in California's Mojave Desert. The message read:

> This pump is alright as of June 1932. I put a new sucker washer in it, and it oughta last five years. But the washer dries out and the pump has got to be primed. Under the white rock, I buried a jar of water, out of the sun and cork-end up. There's enough water to prime this pump—but not enough if you drink some first. Pour in about a quarter of it and let her soak

to wet the leather. Then pour in the rest and pump like crazy. You'll git water. The well never has run dry. But when you git watered up, fill the jar again, and put it like you found it for the next feller.

Signed, Desert Pete.

Who left a water jar for you? Imagine where you would be today if it were not for the ripple effect of God's flowing river of living water.

- Take a drink.
- Fill the jar.
- Pass it on.
- Let the flow continue.

What might happen in your community if you concentrate on your circles of influence and not so much on perfect strangers. Most people have no trouble speaking to persons in their circles of influence!

Let us take a journey through stories related to all seven circles and see if we can make a clear presentation of the powerful influence available to each one of us. The premise is this: Love is meeting needs—and when you meet needs, you will get to share Jesus. The most obvious place we are going to meet needs is in our circles of influence.

SELF

The first circle of influence you have is yourself. There is a flow to life. This living water flows to us and then through us. When Jesus calls us to follow, He calls us to die to self, to *me*, to *my*, and to *mine* and let Him be Lord of our lives. The vertical relationship of you

SOAKING UP THE INTERRUPTIONS

and the Father is most important. When the daily relationship between the Christian and the Father is sweet, fresh, and growing, then horizontal relationships are better and best.

It is nearly impossible to be out of sorts with self or with others and be the vessel through which the living water flows. The water gets stuck. I know. I've been there! Love cannot flow through selfishness, hate, greed, insecurity, or anything else that separates us from the fragrance of Christ. That is why it is critical to keep a balance in life; drink in the living water and pour out the living water.

David, the man after God's own heart, cried out, "Create in me a clean heart, O God, and renew a steadfast spirit within me" (Ps. 51:10). I call that "heart matters." Make this your prayer: "Lord, cleanse me and flow through me to my circle of concern."

Think of the vertical relationship—the renewing—as a process, literally a never-ending process.

FAMILY

Working to keep self in balance, *we move to the second circle: family.* For me today, that's Bob and me (those who live under your roof). *Family* could include extended family of parents or even returning children and, in some households, grandchildren! It seems easier for some of us to try to meet the needs in China than to take care of those in our own homes, the very basis for building relationships. This is the most exciting—and the hardest—area. People in the immediate family know best your strengths and weaknesses; they even know what buttons to push. They have your number and call it often—at just the worst times!

We must be real at home. In what other place can we treat people the worst and still receive love? Nowhere!

When Melody was age four, she said to me after I yelled at her on the way home from a long day at church: "Mommy, how come at church you smile and talk so nice to everyone and you talk so ugly to me and David?" Ouch! See what I mean? Showing love in family can be difficult.

If any one thing could make a difference in the family, I believe it would be the art of listening—not *selective* or *interruptive* listening, but *heart* listening. Look at the person speaking so you can read their feelings as well as hear their words. This is difficult because it takes more time than interruptive listening. I was rolling out bread dough one afternoon, up to my elbows in flour, as my son, David, a second grader, sat eating an afternoon snack and telling me the events of the day. I heard him say, rather exasperatedly, "Look at me when you listen, Mother!" I did.

David gave me another lesson in listening when he was in ninth grade. In March of that year in 1980, I took a position with the Southern Baptist Home Mission Board (now called the North American Mission Board). I commuted between Birmingham and Atlanta for six months while Melody finished her senior year of high school, David, his ninth grade in junior high, and Bob, the final semester of teaching music at Samford University.

It was a difficult time for me. I had to learn a new city and a new ministry . . . and live alone during the weekdays. I was really homesick in the second month at work, so I drove home on a Thursday afternoon instead of Friday to surprise my family. I planned my trip so that I could get there in time to pick up David from school. I was there on time, to be sure. When I saw him come out of the building, I honked the car horn loud enough for the whole world to hear. I saw his head come up. He knew that horn! He began running toward me. I got out of the car just in time to be picked up and swung around by my ninth-grade son! We hugged and hugged. As I got back in the car, I began to cry.

"What's wrong, Mom? You're home! What's the matter?"

I responded through my tears: "I get so lonely all week by myself in Atlanta. I really miss you and Dad and Mel." I thought he would say "We miss you too, Mom!"—but he didn't. He got real quiet. Finally he spoke.

"Mom, when you get home every weekend, you just talk and talk about everything going on in your work and all the people you meet and see. Dad really misses you so much. Dad is so sad with you gone. It's like he's dead or something, and he's no fun at all!"

Wow! Not only was I not listening, I was talking fast and loud—so Bob would not know how frightened and alone I was. I thought if I pretended I was okay, he wouldn't worry about me so much. I had no idea that it was having the opposite effect on him. Once again, my child taught me about listening with the heart. You can be sure I got his message. I got home and farmed out the kids and had Bob all to myself all evening. That night I was honest with Bob. We both were honest about our real feelings and fears. What a great freedom. That gave us the power to cope with the next months before the family finally moved to Atlanta.

Heart listening helps you discern the need, and *love* listening helps draw you to meet some needs so you can be the love of Christ. A woman in Dr. Oscar Thompson's class was challenged by the teacher's words, that meeting needs leads to being in the presence of Christ. As she returned from class, all set to meet needs in love, she encountered a sink full of dirty dishes, clothes all over the floor, and her husband sitting, feet propped up on the furniture, totally engrossed in the paper. Her instinct was to go on a rampage! Been there?

With Dr. Thompson's words fresh in her heart, she greeted everyone kindly, began to pick up the mess in the kitchen, and asked her husband if he would be so kind as to start the bathwater for the children while she did the dishes. She heard the water running and then the voices of laughter. By the time she finished her job, her husband had bathed the children and had them ready for bed. She told Dr. Thompson the next day, "It works! It really works." When you meet needs in love, you are sharing Christ.

Imagine the difference you can make in your family when you realize your circle of influence has the possibility of bearing fruit that remains. Read the words of Jesus in John 15:16: "You did not choose Me, but I chose you, and appointed you, that you should go and bear fruit, and that your fruit should remain, that whatever you ask of the Father in My name, He may give you."

Consider this as a *divine appointment:* chosen to bear fruit that remains. What a great invitation—to join Christ in Kingdom work. Consider this a promise to have His authority to use His name in prayer for those encounters in everyday family situations.

When children see their mother make a sacrificial decision in their behalf, they have seen Christ's love. When a wife hears a husband pray over making difficult extended family choices, she sees Christ's love. When children see parents expressing tenderness toward each other, disciplining in love, and working together, they see Christ's love as needs are met. Cherish the circle of family in prayer, and open your heart to seeing all God can do in your family.

An area of great interest to me is for parents to pray for the salvation of their children. Please do not leave this responsibility to the church! It is the responsibility—and privilege—of the parents. Today, as a grandmother, my circle grows as now I pray that my grandchildren will come to know Christ.

RELATIVES

The next circle of concern is relatives. That can be difficult, too—like family. It is difficult because we may not live close enough to visit and have daily influence. Or it can be difficult because we may live too close and they know all about us! We can pray that God will give us the opportunity to be Christ to those close by and to share Christ with those far away. Consider the task given to us in Acts 1:8 as a divine assignment: "You shall receive power when the Holy Spirit has come upon you; and you shall be My witnesses both in Jerusalem, and in all Judea and Samaria, and even to the remotest part of the earth."

Think of this verse in the context of family, neighborhood, city, state, country, and the world. To meet in love the needs of relatives, we must think about the widening circle, rippling out from us, touching those we seldom see or meet personally, but trusting the Holy Spirit's power through the family of God to show love in circles of need.

As a small child, my favorite uncle, Peter, was in the Royal Canadian Navy. He looked so handsome in his white middy and sailor hat. I was quite sure that when I grew up I would marry him. While at my grandmother's home one summer, my cousin and I waited each day for him to come home. We never knew the exact day, so while we waited we would swing on the garden gate for a portion of each day. When we saw him coming up the alley, off we would go. After hugs and kisses, he would make us close our eyes while he took our gifts from his pocket and put them behind his back. We then went through the ritual of which hand held the gift. Little did we suspect that whatever hand we chose, there was always a gift!

When I became acquainted with the circle concept, I began a family search to discover if all my relatives knew Christ. I assumed that there would be some who did not know Christ as their personal Savior. I was amazed—there were quite a few! I then began talking with my mother and praying with her about her brother, my Uncle Peter, who did not know Him. I came under such conviction because I was traveling around the world speaking to women on the subject of lifestyle evangelism and had an uncle who did not know Christ. First, I began to pray. I asked God what could I possibly do, since he lived in Toronto, Canada. I had not seen him in years and had only kept up with him through Christmas cards. The Spirit whispered to me: *Write a letter.*

I had just finished Gary Chapman's book *The Five Love Languages*, which shows the reader how to communicate in word pictures. Word pictures can conjure up memories to help bring greater communication between persons. The rippling effect caught me at just the right time to reshape my thinking about how to write the letter. I wrote about the great days at my grandmother's house as a child . . . the picket fence . . . the swing . . . the cedar sidewalk . . . the outhouse—complete with the Sears catalog toilet tissue! I recounted the story of meeting Uncle Peter and receiving his gifts. After refreshing his memory with my memory from childhood, I said that I was sorry it had taken so long for me to share with him one of the most important gifts that was ever given to me and to all of mankind . . . God's love through His Son, Jesus. I wrote out for him the Roman road verses about salvation. At the end, I offered him the gift that Jesus gives and wrote out the prayer to pray to receive Christ and invited him to pray that prayer. I sent the letter—covered in my prayers. I did not hear from him for months and months, but I kept on praying.

I was in Glorieta, New Mexico, speaking for a conference and had brought with me my accumulated mail from home. One of those letters was from my mother, and out of the envelope dropped another letter written to her. As best I could make out, someone's relative had died. I called my mother's, asking from whom this letter had come. It was my aunt, my mother's sister. My Uncle Peter had died. I cried out, "Oh, no!"

Mother quickly interrupted, "It's all right. Your Aunt Tootsie has been praying with us for his salvation and, knowing he was very ill, she flew to Toronto to make one last visit to Peter. When she knocked on the door and was let in to his room, she stated the purpose of her visit. He quietly responded, 'That is all settled. I got a letter from Esther.'"

That ripple effect took years. My preacher father had shared the plan of salvation with him more than once, but Peter was not ready. My grandmother, mother, and her sister had prayed for him for years. I joined in prayer—late in the process. God used two authors—Oscar Thompson and Gary Chapman—to bring me to the place of obedience to write the letter. The Holy Spirit managed all those circumstances to bring Peter to Himself. Won't we have a party in heaven—celebrating a homecoming?

FRIENDS

The next circle of concern is friends. It is easy to be in a relationship and talk about absolutely everything . . . except Jesus. Your friends have been put in your circle for a reason. When you meet people's needs through shared friendship, you also will have a chance to share Jesus.

I think often of my son when he was a student at the University of South Carolina where he became involved in a campus ministry group. His freshman roommate was not interested in going with him to the center. David noticed that his roommate had a Bible, but he did not know if he knew Christ, so he asked us to pray that he would live Christ in front of Jim. As they got better acquainted, Jim confessed his loneliness. David said that he was going to Bible study that night and had met some really great new friends. "Why don't you join me?" Not long into the first semester, those campus ministry friends led Jim to Christ. We watched him grow and mature in the faith. He later became the campus ministry president and now is serving as a pastor, continuing that ripple effect of meeting needs in Christ's love.

NEIGHBORS AND BUSINESS ASSOCIATES

The circle continues to move outward and *the next wave flows over neighbors and business associates.* It is still difficult for me to relate this next story because it was a painful lesson for me. When Bob and I lived in Abilene, Texas, we had just purchased our second home on a little lake—well, in West Texas it was maybe just a pond. We had not even had time to paint or change the carpet when the call came for my husband to consider a position on the music faculty as composer-in-residence at Samford University, Birmingham, Alabama. As God directed, we loaded up the cars and began the journey. We stopped that first night at an IHOP (International House of Pancakes) because the children would always eat pancakes. During the meal, Bob said to me, "Did you notice that none of our neighbors came to say good-bye to us?"

I laughed, saying, "Well, George said he would miss David always retrieving his dog from their yard."

Finally at a motel, everyone was in bed and asleep—but me. I heard over and over again the words of my husband about our neighbors not saying good-bye to us. I spent the late-night hours explaining to God why.

I rationalized that we had only lived in that house and small community for four months. I rationalized that we were busy with our small children and many church activities. After all, didn't they see us go out every Sunday, Bibles and Sunday school quarterlies in our hands? That must have counted for something! And every Sunday night, we left with Training Union quarterlies in tow. If they didn't get that, then surely they saw us pack up at 4:00 P.M. every Wednesday to head out to children's choir, mission group, church supper, teachers' meeting, prayer meeting, and adult choir! And if that wasn't enough, I also departed the house every Thursday morning with my bag marked WMU (Women's Missionary Union). Certainly we had left an impression about our lives on our neighbors!

The next morning at breakfast I said to my husband, "I know why."

"You know why what?" he responded. Isn't that like a man—

they never stay with a woman's train of thought! "Why our neighbors didn't say good-bye to us."

"Why?"

"Because we never said hello." You can mark it down. From that moment till now, our neighbors have known who we are . . . and whose we are!

I have come to believe that you do not live in your house because you like the shutters, though I hope you do. Think *kingdom* for a moment. Think *circle of influence.* What does God desire to do through the flow of His love in your life—to meet needs in your neighborhood or office that would have the possibility of drawing someone to Himself?

A friend in Atlanta walks around her neighborhood, praying over the mailboxes as she passes by. When she sees a moving van, she brings homemade soup, introduces herself, and offers assistance. She has had the privilege of leading some of her neighbors to Christ just by meeting needs in love.

The workplace takes much of our time. We are in another circle of concern. As you have lunch, exercise, or attend staff meetings, you have an opportunity to listen for needs so you can share His love.

Christ calls us to Himself in creation, making us that singular, particular fragrance of Himself. The love He pours into us will splash out and be such a sweet fragrance that His love will draw those in our circle to Him. And they will perhaps receive the gift of salvation.

Being a witness is not about a memorized presentation. A great part of splashing the living water that I believe the body of Christ misses is simply talking about the Lord and His reality in our everyday living. I have a friend who, when asked how she is, answers, "I'm blessed—blessed by God's love." In that simple statement, she has blessed God, spoken His name (which is above every name), and may have refreshed another member of the body or made someone thirsty for His blessing. That is part of our responsibility as Christians—to live in such a way that we make the unbeliever thirsty for the living water in us.

After I broke my arm in that skiing accident, I had to go often to the doctor's office for neuromuscular therapy. It was not long until I became acquainted with the receptionist and shared my calling as a Christian speaker—only to discover she, too, is a Christian. With each visit, I answered the doctor's questions about my ministry and I shared my faith with him. He had a religious background. Later another nurse joined the staff. She also is a Christian. In our ordinary conversations, we shared and told each other about our prayer requests from time to time. All three of us began to pray specifically for the doctor.

I moved away from the city, but two years later I received a phone call from the doctor—telling me that he had become a Christian. He didn't even let me ask about it. He just spilled it out. He had asked his receptionist, who he knew was a Christian, if she thought he was a Christian. She replied that she didn't think so because she made some inquiries to which he did not respond. He had pondered her words. The next week he asked another Christian patient if she thought he was a Christian. She not only told him no, but she gave him the same comments! He then called another patient who knew Christ and asked her to come in and lead him to Christ. Our circles overlapped in meeting needs and in prayer—allowing God's Spirit to draw the doctor to Himself.

The story is told of a foreign missionary who moved into a national neighborhood, only to be abused by the locals. Abused, that is, until there was a water shortage and the missionary had the only active well in the community. The missionary saw the need and met the need in love by sharing the well and inviting the rock-throwing nationals to come and get needed water.

A church in Colorado has become known for meeting the

needs of their community. Their premise is that every part of the body gives their gifts to the body in their unique giftedness. One group began a supper club. One couple would clean their home and another couple would prepare the meal. A third couple would serve as official hosts, making sure everyone was acquainted and comfortable. Each of these couples would invite another couple from the neighborhood or workplace with the plan of sharing their relationship to Christ—not through a prepared presentation but in natural conversation.

This activity might happen three or four times during the year, and then the church would host a special dinner evening—complete with a guest speaker and a musician. The supper club group would invite their neighbors and business associates one more time to be their guests. At the end of this evening, there would be a simple, creative presentation of the gospel. The first year's event saw eighty people come to know Christ, because the flow of the river of living water that had been experienced in hospitality.

ACQUAINTANCES

The ripples now move us to the circle of acquaintances. The dictionary says of the word *acquaintance*, "one you know slightly." Perhaps this is the widest area in the ripple effect. Every day our lives move us among acquaintances in the grocery store . . . the airport . . . the PTA . . . the doctor's office . . . the beauty salon . . . the bank . . . your favorite restaurant . . . the Little League ball games . . . the swim club . . . and maybe even . . . the church!

The overwhelming awe I first felt about the circle concept was the awareness that as the circles fan out, they interact with other circles, and the Holy Spirit manages these interacting situations. I may board an airplane and think I am sitting next to Person X— but that may be your neighbor or acquaintance!

I recently boarded an early morning flight out of Jacksonville,

Florida. I sat down next to a woman who was already enjoying her orange juice. I said, "Good morning."

"It is," she responded, "especially if you like what you do."

"You must," I said. She smiled and nodded. I inquired if Jacksonville was her home. She shared she was visiting family and was on business.

When the plane was airborne, I inquired about her family and she asked about mine. Later in the conversation I asked, "What is your business that you enjoy it so much?" She went into great detail about her work with health care issues for women. We were off and running with an easy conversation.

She asked where I was headed. "Out west to speak to a women's retreat." I told her I spoke to women about spiritual heath issues. I shared with her my speaking theme and Scripture, and a story I was using to begin my talk—probably one of my favorite stories.

She grabbed my arm and said, "I can't believe this! You won't believe this!" She reached into her purse and pulled out a "Peace with God" tract. "Last week on a trip, a man sitting next to me shared the same things you are saying. You don't think this is a coincidence, do you?"

You and I, clothed in the Holy Spirit, have His power in us to draw others to Christ—like holy magnetism.

On that plane that morning, I was able to turn a conversation about women's health issues to spiritual health issues, and the Holy Spirit reminded my acquaintance of the little tract in her purse, given to her by someone else involved in the circles of concern.

I couldn't tell her, but I was so fired up that another Christian was being obedient in his circles of influence and that the Holy Spirit gave me an opportunity to be obedient in my circle.

Remember the story of Jesus when He was walking through the crowd and a woman reached out in faith to touch the hem of His garment? He asked, "Who touched Me?" and the disciples said, "Teacher, how could you possibly know in a crowd like this?" He gave them a power-packed answer that they would understand later. "I felt the power leave me."

Have you ever experienced that? Being obedient to the Father, He chooses to use you, and His power changes lives because of your touch. You will feel His power in the situation—which reminds you that it is His power in you—on loan. It will humble and at the same time energize you in His love.

On a trip to Europe with a singing group, Bob and I decided we would take the opportunity to travel in France from Lyons to Paris by the Bullet Train while the choir traveled by bus. We wanted to have the experience and were told we would get to Paris several hours ahead of them and could make the hotel arrangements. We said good-bye to the buses and walked to the train station—only to discover the Bullet Train we needed did not run on Saturdays! The next one would be in two hours. Since we didn't speak French, someone took us to the Travelers Aid waiting room. While sitting there waiting, I noticed a small, demure lady, middle-aged, working quietly behind the desk.

Soon an older woman and a much younger woman entered the room, both crying softly. Their apparel told me they were from India. The woman came from behind the desk. It was obvious she could not speak their language, but the hand motions of the two women told her that they had been robbed. In frustration, the Travelers Aid attendant got them settled and gave them coffee. Then she left the room. She returned with a train station worker from India who could speak the Indian language. Oh, the joy in their eyes as they heard their own language. Through tears, they told the story of stolen money as well as stolen train tickets. I watched as the young man carefully listened to the story and calmly assured them that he would return. He left the room.

The Travelers Aid woman continued to attend to their needs as best she could. Her presence could be felt as she ministered to the troubled ladies. Soon the young man came back into the room, quietly confident. In his hands were two new tickets and money for the journey. The tears . . . the touching . . . and the bowing were a sight to behold. He then took them to their train stop. I was amazed. A total stranger who happened to be from the same country took care of these women, just because of a shared nationalism!

What a portrayal of the gospel that was for me. What a picture of the cross. We come totally lost, unworthy, and with nothing to our name. Jesus takes our lostness and makes it His. He takes His worthiness and makes it ours. He takes His home and makes it ours . . . for eternity. Hallelujah! What a Savior!

I was so curious about this Travelers Aid attendant in Lyons, France. She could speak a little English, and I knew very little French. I had tried to help her assist the ladies by sitting with them as she went for help. After the ladies had left the room, I inquired, with my words and hands, about her volunteer work. I told her I also worked with volunteers, placing them in helping ministries in my country.

She told me her story of the death of an only child. The agony and pain of the experience was still evident on her face. She said, "Finally one day I knew I had to do something to get rid of my pain. I decided I needed to help someone else with life. I came here seven years ago, and I've been here ever since. The only time my pain leaves me is when I am serving here."

Jesus, our wounded healer, calls us to meet needs even through our own pain . . . to meet needs in His love . . . bringing hope to others and to ourselves. What a great mission!

PERSON X

We are now at the concentric circle of Person X. I am amused that Dr. Thompson's book was written in 1981 and we find ourselves in 1998 talking about Generation X, those outside the church who care nothing about denominations but who are asking for guidance in spiritual matters. What a fresh breath of God for you and me who walk beside this generation . . . and can minister to their needs!

The concept of the seven circles is that if each Christian is obedient in their seven circles of concern, there might never be a Person X. Let me illustrate.

Early in the ministry of my father, he would journey into the North Country of Canada every two months to a little village, Chinook Cove, which was a farming community. He preached in a schoolhouse for those who would come to the service. We visited often with the Schmidt family who lived in that community, since my father had led some in that family to know Christ as personal Savior. He had baptized a young man named Allen Schmidt.

Many years later, after completing college and seminary and serving as a pastor in Canada, Allen Schmidt became the executive director of the Canadian Southern Baptist Convention. It has been my privilege to work with Allen and his wife, Katherine, many times in ministry. In 1988, I was making a videotape series related to lifestyle evangelism. I had asked several churches in the area to send women who would be willing to be the audience for this live taping session. In one of the sessions, I asked my audience to turn to their neighbor and share their story of coming to know Christ.

At the lunch break, a beautiful young woman named Sheryalyn approached me. She said that when she came to know Christ, her Canadian pastor asked her to write her name on a piece of paper. Then he asked her to put it in his hands. He closed his hands and asked her to try to get her name out of his hands. She could not. He then told her that no one could ever take her out of Jesus' hand—ever. I thought that was an excellent illustration, but was curious who this pastor was because of my Canadian heritage. I asked her that question and she said, "Allen Schmidt."

I began jumping up and down with excitement. I told her, "My father baptized Allen when he was a teenager!"

A rush of circles flooded our hearts as we both realized this was a wonderful example of the flow of God's love through the circles of concern. My father was faithful in his circle. Allen was faithful in his circle. I was being faithful in my circle as I trained others to meet needs with God's love, and the rippling effect of the circles would continue as Sheryalyn's life flowed out meeting needs and teaching others.

Where do your circles of concern take you, and how do you view each encounter? The real miracle here is that an encounter with life can bring life for another because of the cross. How can we do less than our best in every encounter—thinking kingdom living and splashing the living water on every encounter that is put before us!

Remember, as a Christian you are a living letter in all your encounters.

My prayer is that this chapter has made you look with new eyes at your circles of influence. The Holy Spirit will show you opportunities. You can begin by making a small circle for self and adding six more circles, each one larger than the last. List the concerns of each circle . . . or add names in each area of concern listed below. As you add names, remember these are people already in your circle of influence. Some already know Christ, some need prayer, some need a closer walk with God, and some do not know Christ.

1. Self:

2. Family:

3. Relatives:

4. Close friends:

5. Neighbors/business associates:

6. Acquaintances:

7. Person X:

Begin by praying for each person in your circles of concern:

       Sunday—pray for yourself.
       Monday—pray for your family.
       Tuesday—pray for your relatives.
       Wednesday—pray for close friends.
       Thursday—pray for neighbors and business associates
       Friday—pray for acquaintances.
       Saturday—pray for person X.

You may want to keep this list handy in your prayer journal for continual updates.

MORE SPLASHING: Read Oscar Thompson's *Concentric Circles of Concern* (Nashville: Broadman Press, 1981).

9

SPLASHING THE
LIVING WATER

Some time ago I was flying from Dallas to Knoxville with the usual change of planes in Atlanta. When it was time for my plane to depart Atlanta, I was still in the air—circling because of bad weather. I *had* to make my connection. I said to the stewardess, "I must get off this plane!" I don't know what I thought she might do! Perhaps open a door and let me out?

She calmed me by saying that my connecting plane to Knoxville was probably circling Atlanta also, and she gave me instructions to follow as soon as we landed. Once at the gate, I rushed off the plane, following her instructions. Sure enough, a car was waiting for me at the bottom of the steps!

Once I was in the car, the driver proceeded to take me under the bellies of all those huge planes—from concourse A to concourse D. The driver had me walk up the rear steps that the ground crew uses to care for the plane. As soon as I stepped inside the cabin, the door was shut and the plane was cleared for departure. The airlines do not do this in today's travel, I'm sorry to say. I found my 10-C seat, sat down and, as I buckled up, I quietly said to myself, "Thank You, Father!"

The young man sitting next to me looked my way. "Excuse me. Were you talking to me?"

"Oh, no, sir. I was thanking God that I made this flight connection." Still out of breath from traveling under all those plane bellies, I explained the reason for my expression of thanks: "I am to speak in a Knoxville church in the morning at 8:30 and again at 11:00. I'm also scheduled in another church tomorrow evening and yet another on Monday morning."

He looked at me in puzzlement, and said: "What are you . . . a nun or something?"

I laughed and replied, "Oh, no! I'm a priest!"

I can still see him looking at my collar, or at least looking *for* a collar.

"I could use a priest," he said.

Isn't that just like God—to outdo Himself that evening, to arrange for me to be late, to have a waiting car so I could make this connection, and then to make this divine encounter . . . just so He could bring glory to Himself by allowing me to minister to this hurting young husband and father! The young man began to pour out his heart before the plane even got in the air, telling me that he was going through a divorce and that he had small children who needed him. The hurt in his heart came pouring out as tears in his eyes.

I just love being a grandmother! I believe God uses my grandmother status to encourage and attract younger folk. Maybe they think I have lived long enough to have learned a few lessons. I patiently listened to the rush of his life as he told of trying to get ahead in business, sadly, to the neglect of family and church. He wanted me to tell him what he could possibly do to recapture his marriage and home.

In telling his story, he responded to my questions concerning his faith background. He shared that he had grown up in church, had attended Bible study and knew Christ, but had gotten away from the church. I shared with him my faith journey while encouraging him to go back to church and ask for help there. He said he would do that, and I said I would remember him in prayer, praying that God's love would invade his circumstances in such a way as to bring healing in his family.

After our short flight he said, "I'm so glad you made this plane and sat next to me. I don't think it was an accident."

"Nor do I," I responded with a rejoicing heart for God's kindness in allowing our circles of influence to touch. I am convinced that our world needs more priests—not more pastors! First Peter 2:9 reminds us, "You are a chosen race, a royal priesthood . . . a people for God's own possession."

I made it to Knoxville just fine but, wouldn't you know it, my luggage didn't. At 7:00 the next morning, still no luggage. I am at the age where I'd rather have my makeup than fresh clothes. You can shower-steam your clothes. All I had was a powder compact, lipstick, and the pencil by the phone pad (yes, I did use it on my eyebrows!). I was to be on TV that morning. I promise you, I got on my knees, letting God remind me of my purpose and asking Him to shine through the natural me. As I dumped all the facts on my husband late that night he said, "Oh, honey! Those people didn't know but what you always have the natural look!" Just the word I needed! He was correct.

The next morning a young mother with a small daughter picked me up on our way to the mission meeting. The mother said to the daughter, "Honey, say hello to the missionary." Silence, as the pretty little girl looked me over.

"Please say hello to the missionary. She is going to speak to our mission group this morning."

More silence.

I thought that perhaps I should speak first. As I turned around again to speak to her, she said, "Well, she looks a lot like a mommy to me!" Our world needs mommy doctors, lawyers, teachers, beauticians, CEOs, librarians, and teacher-priests . . . priesting our circles of influence!

How can we live intentionally in the splashing mode? Well, I can't wait to share with you the patterns drawn from John's gospel, the story of the Samaritan woman in chapter four, which detail for us a simple and natural way to splash the living water on our circle of influence.

John 4:3–4 says, "He left Judea, and departed again into Galilee. And He had to pass through Samaria."

PATTERN #1: CROSSING BARRIERS
WITH THE GOSPEL

Jesus went to the city of Samaria, called Sychar, which was near Jacob's well. Jesus was weary from His journey, so He sat down by the well. It was the noon hour. The disciples had gone into town to get Jesus something to eat. A Samaritan woman came to the well to draw her water for the day.

It is difficult for you and me to grasp the significance of this encounter.

She was a Samaritan and He was a Jew. These two groups hated each other. Jews would cross the street, not wanting to be caught in the shadow of a Samaritan. Samaritans were thought to be unclean . . . less than . . . other . . . or whatever degrading name that could be given to them. So why would Jesus speak first?

Jesus was a rabbi. Only men had the privilege of learning from the rabbi. What a rebel this rabbi was! He declared that He came for the sick . . . not for the healthy.

He is the Messiah and she was a sinner. Do you remember when you came face-to-face with Jesus and saw your sin in light of His holiness? Were it not for grace, you and I would not know His amazing grace! What makes it so amazing is that it includes you and me. Certainly the Samaritan women must have melted that day in repentance before the Messiah. I can't wait to meet her in heaven and ask her how she felt the moment He disclosed the truth.

Jesus crossed every barrier possible to reach this woman: gender, racial, cultural, and sacred—any one of which in that day was formidable. Jesus, the living water, not only splashed the woman, but He met the thirst in her life as nothing ever had. He called it living water, a well of water—springing up, gushing out, never-thirst-again, life-giving water!

What are your barriers today? When I ask this question in a seminar, the two most given answers are always *fear* and *rejection*. Some other barriers might be *time, energy, education, social status,* or *attitude*. Perhaps there are other barriers. Remember 2 Timothy 1:7: "For God has not given us a spirit of timidity, but of power and love and discipline." From where do you suppose this fear comes? It comes from the evil one . . . Satan. If he can use your fear of being rejected to keep you from obedience to share Christ, he will do so. I know. I'm reserved, and for a long time I listened to his voice telling me not to say anything about Christ because I was too shy.

I believe that one of the great barriers to witnessing is *disobedience*. I define *lifestyle witness* as "sharing Jesus Christ in the power of the Holy Spirit and leaving the results to God." I'm convinced that many Christians do not share Christ because they think they fail if they do not lead someone to Christ. You fail only if you fail to share!

Do you remember the encounter Jesus had with the rich young ruler in Luke 18? Jesus was obedient to share the story, and the man refused to believe the truth. Jesus walked away, knowing He had been obedient to God. The rich young ruler walked away, knowing he had failed to believe. Think about this. If you share your faith story with someone and they reject your story, they are not rejecting you. They are rejecting Him. Our culture would have us believe that these people reject us.

In light of the gospel, we have been called to die for our faith.

Yet we let fear of rejection keep us from even telling our faith story. When we understand the work of the Holy Spirit, we know it is not our work to lead someone to Christ but it is our task to be a vessel through which the Holy Spirit can work. He, the Holy Spirit, does the drawing to Christ. This became such a freeing truth for my life. I am not in this alone. As my friend Thelma Bagby used to say, "God and me. That's enough!"

I believe another one of the greatest barriers in today's culture is the *church*. When I first began teaching a seminar on lifestyle witnessing, I would ask the audience to write down the names of people who did not know Christ. I watched, and no pencils moved. Then I said, hoping to make them more comfortable, just describe the person. Do they look like a mail carrier? Still no pencils moved. This made me realize a huge truth: Christians make most if not all of their friends inside the church, and they know few lost people.

I would then ask the audience where they had been in the last forty-eight hours. The women responded:

- Beauty shop
- Grocery store
- Hospital
- School
- Church

I then would ask: Were any lost people there? They all nodded their heads. Were there any Christians there? I could see the truth dawn on them. Everywhere they go, they are in a mission field and they are the missionaries, the sent ones, with the good news!

It is my observation that we make friends in the church with those who look like us, dress like us, smell like us, and go to the same schools and clubs. How convenient. How comfortable. How unlike Christ! The church can be a barrier. Some churches offer Bible study, worship, exercise, meals, recreation, trips—making it unnecessary for Christians to do anything outside their own church! We even build huge sports complexes and fields and organize teams within the church and post signs: MEMBERS ONLY. How ludicrous!

Back to our story! The disciples return with food for the Teacher. John 4:27 tells us that the disciples were much like us. They did not recognize the reality and truth right in front of their eyes. The Word says, "And at this point His disciples came, and they marveled that He had been speaking with a woman; yet no one said, 'What do You seek?' or 'Why do You speak with her?'" Consider this. Who marvels at your life because of those to whom you choose to speak?

I watched a story unfold. A group of high school girls from Georgia belonged to a mission organization called Acteens. They told their mission leader they wished to do something with the group that would really make a difference in their lives and in their community. Looking around the neighborhood for a project, the leader discovered a home for unwed mothers very near their church, and the Acteens decided to go for it.

The group introduced themselves to the management and offered help. The manager said, "Just offer friendship. These girls are just like you—except they are pregnant." Those teenage girls discovered other teenage girls ages fourteen, fifteen, and seventeen who were pregnant and feeling alone.

The Acteens began going one afternoon per week after school to offer friendship. The girls from the home asked if they could go to the Acteens meeting at the church. Sure, they said! Why not! Sometime later, those girls decided to go to the Wednesday Youth Bible Study. The Acteens checked it out with the youth group. Again they were given go-ahead. They told the other youth, "When we bring our friends, don't dare look at them."

Can't you just see the kids in that youth group trying not to look at the pregnant girls as they came to the Bible study? You have to love young people. They can be so accepting. The girls then began going to Sunday morning worship. What a sight it was! The youth always sat in the center—right down front in the worship service. Sprinkled among the church youth were these precious pregnant teens. Wow! The church looked like the church . . . a shelter for recovering sinners! I was very proud of our church.

At the Bible study the youth minister announced the upcoming overnight lock-in. The Acteens took on baby-sitting and work projects in order to earn extra money so they could pay the way for their new friends to attend the lock-in. Talk about crossing barriers with the gospel—this was it!

During the weekend, Tonya—who had been kicked out of her home at age fourteen, had lived on the streets and was involved in drugs, alcohol, and sex—learned of God's amazing love through the example of her new friends. She prayed to receive Jesus as her Savior. I happened to be in service the Sunday morning she was baptized. I was sitting with my then college-age son, David. As Tonya came up from the baptismal waters, she almost yelled, "Yes! Yes!" And . . . the body of Christ in our church broke into applause.

I leaned over to my son and said, "The only difference between Tonya and me . . . is that her sin shows, and mine doesn't always show." What a glorious day for Tonya, and for the Acteens—who really wanted to do something positive for the kingdom and crossed barriers to do it. When Jesus crossed the barriers at the well that day, an entire city came to know Him as personal Savior.

PATTERN #2: SHARING THE GIFT
YOU HAVE WITHIN

The conversation between the Samaritan woman and Jesus continues in John 4:10. "Jesus answered and said to her, 'If you knew the gift of God, and who it is who says to you, "Give Me a drink," you would have asked Him, and He would have given you living water.'"

What truth He declared to her! He was speaking of Himself, God's gift of salvation. If you know Jesus, then you have the gift of God within you. That is the gift we are to splash on others. This gift of God within you is not about your spiritual gifts, abilities, or talents, though God uses those. The gift of God within you is His gift of salvation. And out of that relationship you splash the living water.

From the day that I received Christ as a seven-year-old child until today, I have had the gift of God within me. I'm sure you have heard the old song "I'll tell the world that I'm a Christian." I wanted to tell everyone that I belonged to God's family forever. Why is it we soon get away from that childlike first love about sharing Christ?

I was a good witness until my teen years, and then I let being a teenager keep me from sharing my faith. My thinking was to let others see Christ in me, and when they saw the difference, they would ask me about it. The only problem with that thinking is that it does not work. No one has ever asked me about my relationship to God. I had to learn that sharing my faith was not either/or. It is both/and. It was sometimes getting to minister but not getting to share Christ. Other times, it was sharing Christ but not getting to minister. The bottom line is *obedience*. If you can get this in your life, you will see many opportunities to speak and minister in His name.

PATTERN #3: TURNING A CONVERSATION

Jesus was a master in turning a conversation from earthly issues to heavenly issues. In the narrative of John 4:19–24, Jesus and the woman have a religious conversation. She knew the history of Jacob's well. She knew about temple worship in Jerusalem. Jesus, after telling her the most important words of her life—about the living water truth—then tells her another significant fact about true worship. In verses 21–24, He said:

> "Woman, believe Me, an hour is coming, when neither in this mountain, nor in Jerusalem, shall you worship the Father. You worship that which you do not know; we worship that which we know, for salvation is from the Jews. But an hour is coming, and now is, when the true worshipers shall worship the Father in spirit and truth; for such people the Father seeks to be His worshipers. God is spirit, and those who worship Him must worship in spirit and truth."

Most of us are good with religious conversation. We talk about our church or Bible study. We talk about our denomination or about a certain speaker. That is just religious talk. That is not splashing the living water. Splashing the living water is making someone thirsty for the living water—then offering the cup of living water that Jesus so freely offers.

Many people in our world are comfortable having a conversation about religion or about God. It is quite a different thing to converse about Jesus and His saving power. Most people know something about God. The issue is this: Do they know about God's work through His Son on the cross?

Don't be discouraged if you are at the place where you can only have religious conversations. That is a beginning, and you can ask God to help you begin to learn to turn a conversation and to be able to give a word of testimony and lift up the name of Jesus and move the conversation to eternal truth. In telling someone about your weekly Bible study, turn the conversation to share why it is important in your life to go to Bible study and seek to learn eternal truths by which to live—which may lead to your getting the opportunity to ask this person to join you in Bible study.

At 5:30 one morning, I was picked up by the airport van in

Oklahoma City. As the gentleman took my luggage and put it in the van, he asked me on what airline would I be traveling. I told him Delta. He then said, "Well, you must be going to Atlanta." I guess he had the early morning run and knew the Delta schedule.

"Yes, I am—and you know what they say about Atlanta!"

"No. What do they say?" he responded.

"They say if you're going to heaven, you've got to go through Atlanta. Just between you and me, that's not really what they say. They say if you're going to (pointing down) you must go through Atlanta."

The gentleman replied quickly, "You know, lady, there's only one way to heaven—and that is through the cross of Jesus Christ." I had tried to turn a conversation, and he turned it to the truth. Since we were kin in Christ, I moved up to the front seat, and we shared Christ all the way to the airport. He took my luggage all the way to the Delta counter. (I gave him a good tip.) He gave me a hug. God smiled as an African-American gentleman and a grand-mother hugged in Christ that morning. My new brother-in-Christ knew how to turn a conversation that lifted up the Savior!

Another time I was once again at the airport. I chose to ride the cart from gate 3 to gate 33—which is a long way at the Dallas International Airport! At one of the stops, a priest got on the cart and sat down by me. He asked cheerfully, "Is Dallas your home?"

I was startled and tried my best to remember where I lived at the moment! You might say I was having a senior moment. Bob and I had just moved to Florida. "No," I finally stumbled.

"It's not mine either," he said. "Mine is Cloud 22."

"If yours is 22, then mine is 23!" He laughed with me, and gave me the high five!

"Praise God. Then you know Jesus!"

I said I did. We splashed the living water all over the cart that day as we talked about our relationship to Jesus. My suspicion is that perhaps this priest rides the cart all day—every day—just splashing folks with the same question and hoping for the same answer. I smiled, thinking about the refreshment he was to my life. Ask God to teach you to learn to turn the conversation and to bring glory to the Father.

PATTERN #4: CONFRONTING THE SIN

The story takes a turn just after Jesus shared with the woman that He can give her life-giving water like a well, springing up to eternal life. The woman responded, "Sir, give me this water, so I will not be thirsty, nor come all the way here to draw" (John 4:15).

Watch the turn in conversation in verse 16: "He said to her, 'Go call your husband, and come here.'" What did Jesus know that led Him to ask about her husband after she asked for the living water? He knew her thirst. I picture this woman caught once again by her lifestyle, hanging her head and quietly answering, "I have no husband" (v.17). Just imagine with me what might have happened. Jesus may have reached toward her, lifted her chin so their eyes could meet, and tenderly said, "I know, daughter. You have bravely told the truth. Can we talk about your husbands? Can we talk about your thirst?" The Scripture really says, "The woman said to Him, 'Sir, I perceive that You are a prophet.'"

Jesus modeled for us another pattern—confronting the sin. I believe it was at the moment that Jesus confronted the woman with her sin that she knew He was the Messiah. I believe that when Jesus looked into her eyes with His words, He saw her sinful heart. She must have been awakened to her sin as he detailed so vividly her background.

As you move about in your circle of concern, you will have some situations that as you develop the relationship, like Jesus you must confront the person with the cost of sin and the eternal separation resulting from sin.

We cannot tell a person all about Jesus—and never tell them

that "the wages of sin is death, but the free gift of God is eternal life in Jesus Christ our Lord" (Rom. 6:23). I perceive this as different from getting in someone's face and saying something like, "If you die tonight, do you know if you would go to heaven or hell?"

Dr. Roy Fish, a Texas Baptist Seminary professor, gave me this tool for confronting the sin. He suggests that you say, "Has anyone ever told you who Jesus is, or would you say you are in the process of discovering who He is?" I feel very comfortable with this statement and find it works for my personality. This whole concept of splashing the living water is individualized by your personality, your spiritual gifts, and your communication style—all under the obedience of the heavenly Father. He does not ask me to share as Billy Graham does. I couldn't. I'm Esther Burroughs. The same is true for you.

This means that at times, you will find yourself doing what you thought you could not do. As I first began to travel, my friend Ruth Ward heard me teach, telling that I was shy and that it was hard for me to go door to door to present the claims of Christ. As an author about personality types, she came to me privately and said, "You are not shy. You are reserved, and there is a difference. You can draw a reserved person into a conversation by finding out an interest. That will help them open up."

That was such good news to me. I had used my shyness to keep from sharing Christ. As a reserved person, I realized I usually let the other person take the lead in a conversation, which felt comfortable and easier for me than sharing my relationship to Christ. As a reserved person, if you ask me questions about things I'm interested in, I will open up and talk.

Ruth continued, "By the way, as you travel and share Christ on Delta Air Lines, that is just like going door to door!" I now recognize that a Delta Air Lines plane is my personal neighborhood and office.

Let me illustrate this pattern. Being obedient to the Spirit's leading and minding my own business . . . lap table up . . . Bible open and notebook in hand . . . ready to study and write, I study while waiting for the plane to take off. On a recent trip, a man sat down in the seat next to me. He reached out and grabbed my arm and said, "Hey babe! How ya doing?" Well, I'll tell you that my body stiffened! No one calls me "Babe," but *my* Babe. My voice and body language gave a brief and cool greeting, and I turned back to my work. As he settled into his seat, he touched my arm again, babbling on about the weather. I thought to myself that maybe I should show him my granddaughter photos. Then he would leave me alone. I acted very busy with my notebook, hoping he would leave me alone. He continued to chat as he eyed my Bible.

"How long you been religious?"

Still acting cool, I said, "I grew up in a minister's family and came to know about God's love as a child."

"Well, how about that!" he laughed. "I just bet you go to church all the time and really believe in all that stuff."

By now, I'm thinking he is either thirsty for the living water or is making fun of me, so maybe I need an attitude adjustment. As soon as the plane leveled off, the flight attendants began to serve the meal. I accepted the meal, but he said, "Oh, no, I have big plans for the evening!"

As I received my meal, I put my Bible in my lap, bowed my head and, as I usually do, gave the blessing for my meal. As I lifted my head, he said quietly, "Oh, you're very religious!"

Looking at him for the first time, I replied, "It is a habit I learned in my childhood, and I can't imagine not thanking God for everything He gives, and besides I asked for a safe journey home."

His next action caught me completely off guard. He leaned over and took my Bible off my lap. I raised my eyebrows and thought about getting off the plane somehow! But then I caught my breath. He was thumbing through the pages of my Bible, seemingly looking for a Scripture. At that moment, the Holy Spirit whispered to me, *Help him.* I don't know if you talk back to the Spirit, but I do, and I explained to the Spirit that this man was the same man who touched me and called me Babe. Again, I heard, *Help him.*

But I just don't . . . in my arguing with the Spirit, I heard myself say, "Bill [I'd learned his name by this time], may I help you?" He pulled a scrap piece of paper from his pocket and as he handed it to me, he said, "I've been looking for a Bible for six months."

My dear Jacksonville friend Linda Montgomery, in our prayer group at the church, would say, "Don't you just love it when God shows off?" What a flowing river event for me—sitting there as a living Bible (a living letter, Paul says) and with a physical Bible available at God's disposal.

Bill showed me the slip of paper and handed me my Bible. I noted the Scripture and looked it up for him. Being a woman, I read it, noting it spoke about forgiveness, and then I passed the Bible back to him, showing him the verse. He read in silence but could not keep his tears back. He began to weep and said, "I'm having an affair." Caught off guard again, I tried not to show my shock as I was trying to keep from swallowing my tongue! In fast forward I was thinking, *What do I say now? Are you having a good time? How is it going? Oh, my! Does your wife know?* Not to worry . . . he spoke first.

"My daughter is a Christian like you, and she wrote my wife a letter, and I read it. My daughter asked my wife to forgive me and to let us start over."

He never even took a breath. He fast forwarded the story.

"But I don't want to stop the affair, and I don't want to lose my family. I'm embarrassed to tell you that my wife is like you. She loves God and her Bible. She's a Christian, just like you, and I've ruined her life. Do you think she could ever forgive me?"

He really didn't mean for me to answer, and he kept on talking.

"My children hate me. I'm about to destroy my life. I'm so

ashamed. I'm embarrassed to tell you I am a Christian—just like you—and I know I'm wrong."

Wow! Now I knew how to answer.

"Bill, do you know why you are crying? You have broken God's law. When you break God's law, it breaks God's heart. His desire is that we live in fellowship with Him, but when we sin, we break that fellowship. It feels like hiding from His holiness."

"I know," he cried.

I was amazed at myself—talking with passion to this man, whom I had all but ignored, and being bold enough to talk about his sin! That is how the Spirit leads us—even when we do not want to be led. I tried to explain to Bill that his daughter was trying to give her mother the same message. On our journey through life, we will all sin. But God's forgiveness at the cross is forever . . . past, present, and future.

I told Bill that he needed to repent of his sin, confess it to God, and then confess to his family and ask for their forgiveness. I assured him that God's love was so powerful that this sin could be forgiven and even forgotten and that God was capable of putting his marriage back together in such a way that God would receive glory!

As he wept, I felt helpless and wished for a godly man to be sitting close by who had great words of wisdom. As the plane was landing, I reached into my purse to give him a tract to reinforce what I had shared with him. As I picked it up, my hands opened it to the page that illustrated repentance and forgiveness. Well, perhaps it wasn't *my* hand at all . . . but I said, "Bill, here it is. *Repent* means to turn away, to walk away from the sin, to accept God's forgiveness, and to start over." He thanked me as we got off the plane together, and as I walked away, he called out, "Esther! Pray for me!" I did and I continue to do so.

The next morning in staff meeting as the group shared, I told them the story that you have just read. I said, "If only one of you guys had been sitting beside Bill, it would have made a difference."

A friend in the group quietly said, "He probably would not have told a man what he told you." Yes! God chooses to work through women as He calls us in relationship to Himself. Bill may have been a Person X in my circle of influence, but his daughter was already involved in ministry to him.

Be open to God choosing to use you to lovingly confront others with the good news of forgiveness and new life.

PATTERN #5: LIVING WATER REPLACES PHYSICAL AND SPIRITUAL HUNGER

I imagine Jesus' conversation with the Samaritan woman took some time when you consider the length of the conversation plus the fact that Jesus was not in a hurry since His disciples had gone to town for food. I usually say they had gone for a Big Mac! John 4:27 tell us that the disciples came and marveled that Jesus "had been speaking with a woman; yet no one said, 'What do you seek?' or, 'Why do you speak with her?'" The disciples were mostly concerned with meeting Jesus' physical needs with the food they had brought back. They kept insisting He eat. "Rabbi, eat" (v. 31).

Jesus said to them, "I have food to eat that you do not know about" (v. 32). Verse 33 relates their confusion. "The disciples therefore were saying to one another, 'No one brought Him anything to eat, did he?'" You have to laugh. They thought they were in charge of His eating. They were concerned that someone else had brought food to the Teacher before they had gotten back from town. Listen to His answer . . . it is profound for us to hear in today's overscheduled culture of one-minute managers and micro-managers, always on top and in control of the situation! Translated literally, Jesus said, "I have just eaten of God." No wonder He walked through the gospel of John calling Himself the Bread of Life. In John 6:35, Jesus said to them, "I am the bread of life; he who comes to Me shall not hunger, and he who believes in Me shall never thirst." The Bread of Life shared the living water with the woman—feeding her soul and fill-ing His. He was so full spiritually that He was not hungry physically.

Don't be surprised. That is exactly what you and I feel when we have a chance to share the living water with someone. "So the woman left her waterpot, and went into the city, and said to the men, 'Come, see a man who told me all the things that I have done; this is not the Christ, is it?'" (John 4:28–29).

Do you suppose she forgot the waterpot in the excitement of the disciples' return? Or because she had such good news to share? Or having received the whole well of living water, she no longer needed a waterpot? Perhaps all three. Imagine the confusion in the town at her news.

- The thoughts of the men who knew her so intimately
- The women's astonishment at her announcement
- Her joy in her new relationship with Jesus
- Her delight in introducing her village to Jesus

The story tells us: "And from that city many of the Samaritans believed in Him because of the word of the woman who testified, 'He told me all the things that I have done'" (v. 39). The living water replaced the physical and spiritual hunger. The Word can do that for you and me . . . even today.

Consider this: when the disciples went into the village, they only brought back food. When the woman went into the village, she brought back the entire village. The disciples, who knew the Bread of Life, went for physical bread. The woman, who had just met the Bread of Life, brought the hungry to the Bread of Life whom she knew as the living water. Perhaps it was just a chance encounter. A divine encounter, more likely. One Messiah. One Samaritan. One village—splashed by the living water—forever changed because of one woman's thirst.

Some time ago I had flown following a storm up the east coast. I barely made my connection through the Atlanta airport, but I made the speaking engagement with no trouble. After speaking that night, I got to the hotel and unpacked my luggage. It was Valentine's weekend, so I was not surprised to find a card hidden in my luggage. I smiled at what my husband had written: "When you get home this weekend, we'll party [dot, dot, dot]." Well, I thought about those dots all weekend and couldn't wait to get home.

After teaching the next morning, I made my way to the Harrisburg, Pennsylvania, airport—in seven inches of snow, and not the least concerned about my flight. After all, they know about snow in the North. I laid my ticket down on the counter and waited for the attendant to check my bag. He said, "Mrs. Burroughs, this flight is canceled."

"It can't be," I protested.

"Well, it is! See that sign?"

"You don't understand! I'm on my way home to dot, dot, dot!"

He looked at me as if he did not understand—and I was not about to explain! "When is the next flight?"

"Four hours from now," was the reply. Then he said, "By the way, you have a ticket from Harrisburg to Atlanta—but not one from Atlanta to West Palm Beach." This was too much bad news for a little gal who had just had her Valentine's party canceled. After searching my purse, the tears began to flow. He said, "Let me look this up." As he did, I am sure he saw I was a platinum level Delta frequent flyer. He smiled and said, "Let me fix that ticket for you."

I cried some more. Tears work for me! Four hours to wait . . . getting home past midnight. Small plastic chairs for comfort . . . coffee from a machine . . . not looking good. I called home. "Hey, Babe! Glad to hear from you. How ya doing?"

"Not good," I teared.

"What's the matter?"

"Tell me I love what God's called me to do?"

"You *do* love what you are doing! Why?"

"My plane has been delayed and I won't get home till midnight!"

"No problem," he laughed. "We'll just party at midnight!"

That's a problem, you see. *I don't party at midnight!* Maybe 9:30, or maybe 10:00 . . . but not midnight! Receiving his encouragement, we said good-bye.

Boarding the crowded plane four hours later, I took my seat by a young couple. Settling in, I asked the young woman if she lived in Harrisburg. Patricia grew up in the area, but now lived in West Palm Beach and was back home for her grandfather's funeral. My mother's heart was immediately touched. I expressed my sadness for her, and she began telling me about being raised by her grandmother. I listened. She told me how, as a small child, she had learned Bible verses and songs from her gramma, and had gone to church all her life. "She taught me that Jesus loved me. She led me to love Jesus."

"What a great faith heritage you have," I said. I shared a little about my childhood home, and we both acknowledged that we had faith in Christ.

Then she whispered, pointing to her husband, and said "But he doesn't." Isn't that just like a woman? We'll tell everything! We talked a long time about her grandparents. She needed a listening heart and a strong shoulder upon which to lean. I asked her what church they attended in West Palm Beach. She told me they were newlyweds and hadn't started church yet. Then I gave her my grandmother advice, sharing how important the body of Christ is to newlyweds as they establish their marriage.

As Patricia and I talked about the church, her young husband, Mike, leaned over in front of her and said, "That man yesterday at the funeral . . . the, ah, pastor. Yes, the pastor talked about a 'shepherd' leading us."

I said, "Did he talk about 'the Lord is my shepherd, I shall not want. He makes me to lie down in green pastures; He leads me—'"

"Yes," he interrupted! "That shepherd! Do you know the shepherd?"

All of a sudden I knew why my flight had been canceled. I told him about the Great Shepherd of the Twenty-third Psalm, and how as a small girl I had understood His willingness to send His Son to die on a cross and God's love for me. I told him how I had learned that this Great Shepherd wanted to be *my* Shepherd—and Friend through the rest of my life.

Then Mike asked me a question that stopped my heart. "If you've never been in a church in all your life, how do you get in one?"

I smiled, knowing I couldn't wait to tell "dot, dot, dot" about this young man. I told Mike, who by now was leaning across his wife and quietly listening to my words, the story of the shepherd who had ninety-nine sheep in the pen but who had one sheep missing. The shepherd went looking for that one lost sheep. "It is the Great Shepherd's work to look after His sheep and guide them," I told him. "He is the kind of Shepherd who knows every sheep by name.

"Mike, all you have to do to get to know this Shepherd is to confess your lostness and accept His love for you, which will admit you into the fold of the Shepherd's family forever."

His eyes filled with tears as he listened. Patricia added her voice as she cried about her grandfather, whom she knew had gone home to the Good Shepherd. The presence of the Holy Spirit was so real in our conversation. Mike agreed he would think about the Shepherd's invitation. As we exited the plane they both thanked me for sitting by them, and they promised they would find a church. I gave them the name of one church near them. I knew the pastor as a friend and said I would call him and tell him this story.

I got off the plane just dancing. I know that's not Baptist . . . or Nazarene . . . but it is very biblical. King David, the shepherd king who loved the Good Shepherd, danced before the Lord. My husband was there to meet me with a bouquet of flowers, and I'm sure he was expecting me to be dragging in. Was he ever surprised! I hugged him furiously!

"What happened to you?" he asked.

"Let me introduce you to Patricia and Mike."

Bob smiled knowingly.

Often I find myself submitting to circumstances beyond my control and wondering why—knowing I will be shown the reason. How wonderful that God continues to be as patient with us as with the disciples. All they were thinking about was physical food; all I thought about was getting to West Palm Beach on time for "dot, dot, dot." Kingdom living is rich. I miss it so often as I plow ahead with my own agenda, thinking it's all about on-time airplanes and being surprised by funeral attenders and a need for the Shepherd. I'm glad for the touch of love that allowed this encounter of encouragement and spiritual food to my own heart.

PATTERN #6: SOWING AND REAPING WILL ENLARGE THE KINGDOM

The dialogue at the well continued. "Already he who reaps is receiving wages, and is gathering fruit for life eternal; that he who sows and he who reaps may rejoice together" (John 4:36).

The Teacher pointed out a wonderful truth at the well that day. It has the power to free you to splash indiscriminately . . . guilt free . . . result free. Free! FREE!

Jesus gave equality to sowing and to reaping. Evangelical Christians tend to do just the opposite and make reaping *the* most important part of the experience. Not Jesus! He stated that the sower and the reaper rejoice together. That must mean they work together! What wonderful news! I can celebrate when the Spirit draws a person to Himself—through me. And I can celebrate, whether I am the sower of the seed or the harvester in the field. Keep in mind that the harvest is not the end of the meeting or event . . . it is the end of the age. And He is the Harvester. We are His field hands. The field is His, and we work the fields in joy together, knowing He will ultimately bring in the harvest.

What an affront it must be to Jesus when we refer to *my* Bible study or *my* mission project or *my* choir. Does He cover His eyes and wonder if we will ever understand kingdom authority?

One of my favorite days in Oswald Chambers' *My Utmost for His Highest* is September 6. It is titled "Rivers of Living Water," John 7:38.

> A river touches places of which its source knows nothing, and Jesus says if we have received of His fullness, however small the visible measure of our lives, out of us will flow the rivers that will bless to the uttermost parts of the earth. We have nothing to do with the outflow—"This is the work of God that ye believe. . . ." God rarely allows a soul to see how great a blessing he is.
>
> A river is victoriously persistent. It overcomes all barriers. For a while it goes steadily on its course, then it comes to an obstacle and for a while it is baulked, but it soon makes a pathway round the obstacle. Or a river will drop out of sight for miles, and presently emerge again broader and grander than ever. You can see God using some lives, but into your life an obstacle has come and you do not seem to be of any use. Keep paying attention to the Source, and God will either take you round the obstacle or remove it. The river of the Spirit of God overcomes all obstacles. Never get your eyes on the obstacle or on the difficulty. The obstacle is a matter of indifference to the river which will flow steadily through you if you remember to keep right at the Source. Never allow anything to come between yourself and Jesus Christ, no emotion, or experience; nothing must keep you from the one great sovereign Source.

Think of the healing and far-flung rivers nursing themselves in our souls! God has been opening up marvelous truths to our minds, and every point He has opened up is an indication of the wider power of the river He will flow through us. If you believe in Jesus, you will find that God has nourished in you mighty torrents of blessing for others.

Our lives are to be a channel through which the love of Jesus can flow. Keeping the focus of our lives on Jesus Christ allows the continual flowing of God's power through us. John 7:38 teaches: "He who believes in Me . . . from our innermost being will flow rivers of living water."

We can pray, God, make me obedient . . . to drink in a stream of the living water, and splash out the living water so that others become thirsty, desiring to drink of the living water. The well is not an end of itself, but becomes the source from which a river flows.

Stacy, my neighbor, wanted a relationship with Jesus. I showed her John 3:16 and shared how my teacher had shown me as a child that the *whosoever* meant me, by name. I shared how I prayed, asking Jesus into my heart, and accepted His gift of eternal life. It was as if the light dawned, and questions about this new relationship poured out. It was fun to watch Stacy's thirst for Him be satisfied in the Word. Our walks became discipleship times. The struggles were still there, but now His love was there, also.

A year later, I was flying back to Atlanta where Bob and I lived at the time. My seat was by the window, and a man was already in the aisle seat, thoroughly engrossed in a book. A vacant seat was between us. He did not look up or speak as I got to my seat. Some time later, as the meal was served, he placed the book in the seat between us. I glanced at the title, *Codependent No More*, by Melody Beattie. I casually said, "Good book you're reading!"

"You know this book?"

"I do."

"Well, I've just been home to visit family. I am getting things sorted out. What I really want is to be empowered."

"I know a little about that, also. I just wrote a book called *Empowered*."

"I'd like a copy, if you don't mind."

"I don't have it with me, but if you give me your card, I will send you a copy when I get home."

"Great. Where do you live?"

"Atlanta," I said.

"Me too. Where in Atlanta?"

"I live in Lullwater Estates—off Ponce."

"So does this woman in my office—and she is *empowered*. All of a sudden, she brings our staff together and she prays over decisions."

"What work do you do?" I inquired.

"I'm a graphic artist."

"Really? What company?"

"Lewis, Clarke, and Graham."

Hesitant, I asked, "Do you know Stacy?"

"That's the woman I'm talking about!"

"She's my neighbor," I laughed.

"Then you must be Esther! She talks about you all the time." Wow!

Safely home, I unlocked my front door, putting down my luggage. The phone was ringing. It was my neighbor, Stacy. "Bob just told me he met you on a Delta airplane!"

"It's true."

"Wow," she said! "Now there are two of us talking to him about the Lord."

"Three," I reminded her. "Who but God could have arranged these circumstances!"

Women, choose to live in the expectancy of how the Holy Spirit will manage the circumstances of your life giving you joy in Splashing the Living Water!

SPLASHING ON YOUR WAY . . .
OUT OF YOUR WAY

1. What about your life cannot be explained, apart from the Holy Spirit?

2. Does your lifestyle make others thirsty to know the joy of the living water?

3. Would you consider living in such a way as to choose deliberately splash the living water?

4. In your relationships with other people, is there an eternal impact because of the fragrance of Christ in your life?

MORE SPLASHING: Pray this prayer right now, "God, make me obedient in my walk to splash the living water till others develop a thirst and come to drink. Amen."

ABOUT
THE AUTHOR

Esther Burroughs currently serves as the director of "Esther Burroughs Ministries . . . Treasures of the Heart," a speaking and writing ministry. She and her husband, Bob, have been married 40+ years—writing musicals, traveling, and just being together through the years in ministry. Esther's great delights include the honor of being "Nana" to four grandgirls and one grandson, doing needle work, gardening, and dining out with her sweetheart.

She began her speaking career in 1972, serving as Campus Minister at Samford University in Birmingham, Alabama. She has continued her ministry as a speaker for the past 27 years to audiences ranging from local church congregations, overseas audiences, women's conferences and college students.

Esther Burroughs—an author, writer, speaker, and grandmother—has a passion to know God and to inspire women to intimacy with God that leads them to touch their world—with His love.